ESTABLISHING A TRAINING FUNCTION

Establishing
a
Training
Function

•

A Guide for Management

•

Charles C. Denova

Educational Technology Publications / Englewood Cliffs, N. J. 07632

Material from Pigors & Myers, *Personnel Administration,* and from Mort & Vincent, *Introduction to American Education,* © McGraw-Hill Book Company. Material from DePhillips, Berliner & Cribbin, *Management of Training Programs,* © Richard D. Irwin, Inc. Material from *Saturday Evening Post* article by C.F. Kettering © The Saturday Evening Post Company. Material from Bienvenu, *New Priorities in Training,* © the American Management Association, Inc. All material used with permission.

Printed in the United States of America.

Library of Congress Catalog Card Number: 72-122813.

International Standard Book Number: 0-87778-005-6.

First Printing.

This book is dedicated
to
Dolores Theresa Crespo
as
partial payment for
what she did
January 27, 1951.

PREFACE

Large numbers of business and industrial organizations, both large and small, provide some kind of training for their employees. The type of training provided varies from informal learning on-the-job to a highly organized instructional program within classrooms under the supervision of the personnel department or of a special training division.

As a rule, the content of training programs in business and industry is limited to the competencies necessary to increase production or services in the occupation providing the training. Training programs include extension and correspondence courses, cooperative classes, supervisory training, management development, organizational development, and apprenticeship and job training.

This volume is written primarily for the purpose of providing information and ideas for those members of management who have the urge to begin a training program in their organization but need some aid in the battle of convincing their peers to get the training program started. Secondly, this is written for members of top management in enterprises that have an existing training program and who desire to evaluate its structure, organization and impact upon the development of personnel.

Charles C. Denova, Ed.D.
Redondo Beach, California
October, 1970

CONTENTS

ESTABLISHING A TRAINING FUNCTION

1.

Establishing Training Activities

Training in business and industry is a specialized and very practical form of education. Basically, it prepares workers to do their jobs well. To accomplish this it develops skills for effective work, knowledges for intelligent action, and attitudes that bring a willingness for cooperation with peers and with management.

Training not only increases production but, properly conducted, it also increases self-confidence and improves the morale of the workers.[1] Training programs can standardize the methods of doing the work, reduce the amount of supervision necessary, lower the turnover rate caused by unsatisfactory adjustment to a new job, correct mistaken judgment as a result of the hiring interview, and increase the interest in the job because of a more thorough understanding of the task to be performed and its relation to that of other employees.

If management has the point of view that labor is primarily an adjunct to the machine and is to be purchased in the cheapest market, its business enterprise will be ineffective. The available human resources will be wasted and the employees will consider the company undesirable. This in turn will have an impact on recruiting the caliber of personnel necessary for a profitable operation.

Building an efficient labor force requires not only proper selection but also effective development of employees. Employee talents are not fully productive without training. The need for training has been increased by rapid technological changes which create new jobs and eliminate old ones and by the growing importance of semiskilled labor relative to unskilled—the plant labor force must absorb new techniques as they develop. Industry is frequently compelled, particularly during periods of business expansion, to hire unskilled labor and to train the new workers for specific operations or tasks. Many jobs in business consist of tasks which are unique and peculiar to the company. A systematic training program can improve the quality and quantity of work, safeguard machinery, reduce costs, raise employee earnings and morale, and provide an effective means for imparting company policies and regulations. Employee relations are effective only when management realizes that its workers are human beings with a number of drives, who differ in makeup, ability and levels of aspiration.

Management is aware that specialists are required to deal with the technical aspects of the business—design, product, process, equipment, facilities, finance, law and the like. Enlightened management is also aware that experts should deal with the human aspect of the business—the aspect which is most complex, dynamic and volatile.

The employer wants efficient methods of production, high labor productivity, quality workmanship, good morale and industrial peace. The employee wants (among other things) job and economic security, fair wages, desirable working conditions and opportunity for advancement. A training organization can go a long way in creating an environment to contribute to employee development and the enterprise development of which management and labor are an integral part.

SPADEWORK: A MUST BEFORE ESTABLISHING TRAINING

If no formal training organization exists, preliminary groundwork by top management is a must prior to the establishment of a training department. Lack of the preparation on the formal organization level can lead to complete failure of the training department on the informal organization level, even though its organizational structure is good, its objectives are sound, and its staff is highly qualified and capable. On the other hand, thorough preparation could build up momentum strong enough to carry a training staff of minimum ability through the difficult beginning phase.

If training activities were well understood by various levels of management, much of the preparatory spadework would not be necessary. But misinterpretation is easy when training is undefined or poorly and sometimes inaccurately defined. When a new activity comes into the organizational family unannounced and unblessed, there will be resistance and raised eyebrows, especially from those who are jealous of their authority and specialization. Top management needs no other reason to prepare the entire organization for the installation of a training department, long before the personnel arrive to perform their training activities.

PREREQUISITES OF A SUCCESSFUL TRAINING FUNCTION

If training is to be successful, top management must give it sincere support. Top management expresses support by its willingness to hire high caliber staff; by adopting and endorsing sound programs; and seeing that the policies, procedures, methods and programs are put into practice. If management expects results from the training department, it must give responsibility accompanied by authority. This authority must include planning, controlling, coordinating and administering of all education and training activities. The concept of the training department operating as a staff function with no power beyond weak and apologetic advice is a poor one indeed. If training can be thought of as a staff function, then the responsibility of personnel development can be delegated. This type of responsibility determination can be accomplished by an upper management edict.

Establishing the Training Function

There are several steps which should be taken by the training staff (especially the training director) once the training department is established. The following are a few of the more important ones:

1. *Outline the goals and objectives for the training program.* The goals of a training department are to increase the efficiency of the labor force, raise morale, and improve working relationships in the enterprise. A full-fledged training program justifies its existence by improving the effectiveness of employees and lowering labor costs.

2. *Formulate sound training policies.* Well-conceived company policies formulated by the top management with the participation of the training director must be the guide to all training programs. The training policies should be harmoniously integrated with the business goals of the enterprise.

3. *Determine the status of the training administration in the organizational structure.* Set up as a staff department, the training office performs its duties as a service to the entire organization. Operating executives, supervisors and foremen require the expert advice and assistance of the training specialist when dealing with the personnel development aspect of business operations. But it is difficult to be effective if the training director is not a member of the top echelon. A training director cannot plan training to meet a need known only to the top echelon of a company's management.

4. *Develop systems and procedures for maintaining training programs.* The need for a systematic training program has been brought about by the rapid technological changes which create new jobs and eliminate old ones. A systematic training program can be effective in both employee development and organization development.

5. *Provide for training research and evaluation: programs, staff and participants.* To determine if the best, most economical training program is conducted, a diagnostic study of every aspect of the training activities is a must. The evaluation plan can be divided into three major aspects:[2]

a. *An assessment of the change in employee behavior.* Every avenue of employee performance must be examined. There should be an analysis of the employee's progress, and the correlation between training evaluation and supervisory appraisal should be investigated. After the training program, the profit contribution or cost savings must be compared as the results of the change in behavior of the participants.

b. *An analysis as to whether or not the training*

program furthers the achievement of organizational goals. In business and industry, there is *no* other valid criterion for conducting training (single courses or program) except an economic one. Every training effort *must* be analyzed for its potential profit contribution. If the training does not result in a profit contribution or cost savings, the investment in training is not economically justified.

c.   *An evaluation of the training personnel, methods and techniques.* The organization responsible for training must establish a reputation for employing and maintaining a highly qualified instructional staff. Evaluation should be designed into the total program and should start at the time the program is being planned. An analysis plan for the evaluation of training programs in business or industry is not a simple process, nor is it an easy task if the job is to be done completely. But the evaluation job *must* be done.

6. *Become known and accepted personally.* An important step in establishing training programs is the development of a close personal relationship with as many members of the management team as possible—top echelon to first-line supervisor. This action will increase the probability that training ideas and counsel will be accepted. Management not only accepts training programs but also the person. Therefore, the training staff must sell itself. Many a program has failed because of irrational and personal blocks.

7. *Be thoroughly acquainted with all phases of the business.* Each member of the training staff should be thoroughly acquainted with all phases of the business of the enterprise. In order

that the training department can be an effective management tool, it must know the details of what has gone on in the past, and must be acquainted with the goals of the future. Knowledge of the details of company operations is a must so that the training staff can aid in the development and guiding of management and workers toward achieving enterprise goals and objectives.

8. *Become familiar with the organizational processes.* The training director must study the organizational processes of the company. He must have a "feel" for the practices and individuals of the organization, and he must be aware of both the formal and the informal organization structure. Many training programs are slowed because they took into consideration only the formal organization structure.

9. *Recognize the need to promote training.* Unfortunately, once training programs are designed, some training directors wait until requested before doing much with their programs. People do not always recognize what is good for them, and those that do seldom get around to doing much about it. The training staff can do much to provide incentives. Regardless of how well training programs are conducted, they will always need publicity and promotion.

Determining Training Needs

There are probably as many rationales for approaching the problem of determining training needs as there are persons who are concerned with the planning and directing of an enterprise. Objectives should be established in broad areas for the entire company. Unless it is known what it is that the company is trying to accomplish, there is no sound criterion on which to base an inquiry of training need. For training planning, then, a clear understanding of organizational goals is a *must*. Whether or not the enterprise objectives are achieved is a function of many factors in addition to training. However, failure to obtain an objective should be a signal to investigate whether or not training had any relationship to the failure.

Here are five steps that will aid in identifying needs that training will meet:

FIRST: Distinguish between "acquirement"

*(what the employee must
know in order to perform
his job)*

AND "accomplishment"

*(the relative value of his
performance as measured
against a desired standard).*

SECOND: Separate performance objectives

*(what is desired to be
accomplished with the
manpower)*

from performance methods

*(how supervision intends
to manage the manpower
to get the job done).*

THIRD: Distinguish between *deficiencies*
of knowledge

AND *deficiencies of execution.*

FOURTH: Develop *criteria of performance*

AND establish *skill priorities*
upon these criteria.

FIFTH: DETERMINE WHAT KIND OF TRAINING
WILL BEST OVERCOME EACH KIND OF
SKILL DEFICIENCY.

ORGANIZATION OF TRAINING PROGRAMS

Training programs must be designed to fit the needs of the company. The scope will depend upon the nature of its business and operations, the size of the firm, its expansion program, the recruitment needs, and whether the enterprise is centrally or decentrally located. Generally, training programs are divided into two major areas, (a) training for specific jobs and (b) general education. General education for an employee in non-job-related personal needs should be encouraged by the company. In some instances, firms financially aid certain types of non-job-related training and education.[5]

Kinds of Training

A comprehensive training program concerns itself with the development of skill, knowledge and attitude. These three factors make up a training program whether it is directed toward workers, supervisors, executives, or customers. For the purpose of administration, it is important to plan the training programs in each of the somewhat different functional divisions based upon the company's immediate *and* long-range needs. A full, integrated training program can be categorized in the following manner:

1. *Employee Training.* This program includes all types of job training and education offered to employees below the supervisory level.

2. *Supervisor Training.* This area of training programs stresses heavily the skills, knowledge and attitudes necessary to a supervisor.

3. *Executive Training.* This program generally differs from supervisor development mainly in breadth and depth.

4. *Customer Training.* This program includes all manner of training designed for persons requiring skills and knowledge about the company's products or services.

One of the paradoxes of the training movement is that such categorization, in general use, continues in spite of the universal objection to artificial distinctions between employee and supervisor, supervisor and manager, labor and management, and company and customer. Recognizing that this traditional classification is forced, it can be understood why many training programs could actually cut across all organizational lines and integrate with employee, supervisor, executive and customer training.

On-the-job Training. On-the-job training given by supervisors is widely employed because no special training facilities and instructional staff are required. It is particularly suitable under the following conditions:

1. When the number of trainees is small.
2. When the training period is short.
3. When the variety of duties, the complexity of the work process, and the need for special equipment makes other forms of training less suitable.

With on-the-job training, the new employee is stimulated by the actual production situation, and his suitability for the job can be ascertained by a supervisor or competent instructor. The underlying disadvantage is in the fact that in most instances on-the-job training is carried on with little or no planning, and is looked upon by supervision as an interruption in the *normal* work pattern.

Vestibule Training. Vestibule training provides instruction in a classroom environment which is a shop-like setup independent of the production line. A full-time instructor is able to apply good teaching techniques under controlled conditions, and can increase trainee self-confidence. Vestibule training disrupts production less and causes less work spoilage than on-the-job training. A major limitation is the expense of providing duplicate equipment and the cost of maintaining a teaching staff.

Supervisory Training. The training of members of the management team is of paramount importance, and should be a continual process. First-line supervision courses should deal with immediate supervisory problems, and then cover such areas as shop management, company policies, production planning, terms of the union contract, merit rating, safety, and methods of cost reduction.

Executive Training. Candidates for middle and top management positions require intensive training as well as a general business background. The program may include class sessions as well as home study assignments. Off-site courses covering business management, labor relations, corporation finance, and the like are offered by colleges and universities. In addition, assignments can be drawn from trade and technical journals and other selected literature.

Training Activities Must Be Organized

Prior to the implementation of training, it should be obvious that the function of a training department must be highly organized if success is to be maximized. Good management practice indicates that planning is of little value if there is no attempt to organize and control a chosen plan of action. Any training activity that an organization undertakes must be of benefit to the company, or else it should not be attempted. If employee training is recognized as being necessary to the welfare of the organization, this means that it should be carried on only if provision for the measurement of its usefulness to the company has been established.

Top, Middle, or Bottom?

Where to begin training? That is the question that plagues every company. There is probably no single best place to start training. Let it begin wherever there is a need for it, there is recognition of that need, there is enthusiasm among those who need it, and there is a training program that can be organized (or made available) to meet the need.

There is an almost universal belief that employee development *must* start at the top and work itself down. This is of questionable merit since there is a psychological resistance in many executives toward improving their own habits first. Those training administrators who insist that training must always start at the top are expecting gifts from the gods. It's not in the cards. As long as we wait until things are perfect above before we start our own improvement, we will never get started since there is no one among us that is perfect.

Starting with worker skill development goes unchallenged if what is taught is needed, practical and beneficial. Starting manager training at the bottom is reasonable since principles and techniques of supervision must be sold on their merit. By beginning at the bottom, enthusiasm is engendered; the instruction can be tried out and, if found valuable, it is accepted and put into practice. Furthermore, lower levels of management will more easily be led to try new ideas to improve their performance.

Efficiency Through Cooperation

Although a company with a training department in its organization has accomplished a most important step toward more efficient training of its employees, this is not to discourage training activities on the part of the line supervisor. In fact, in a well-managed company, the training staff enhances the training that line managers carry on.

If training programs are planned, organized and developed by the training staff through the cooperation of the line management, then such training programs will have a much better chance for success. In addition to coordination, publicity is necessary. A well-publicized training program enjoys greater prestige among each level of the organization. If it is felt that top management is interested in the training function, then every subordinate level will recognize the need for participating actively. This gives the training program greater acceptance, hence making each program have more impact not only on the workers but also the line supervisors. Therefore, the mechanics of publicity, scheduling of personnel, compensation of training time, and recognition of completion of training must be worked out in advance so that the programs move ahead smoothly.

The Right Capital Equipment

If a training function is to start with an optimum chance for success, it must have the right physical equipment. The efforts of good administrators and good instructors can be scuttled with inadequate facilities. It has been said that education can take place sitting on the end of a log. Not in the business environment of today. Try placing a log near an assembly line or in a bank lobby and see how much learning takes place.

The training environment should be large enough to accommodate the people to be trained. These areas must be well lighted and well ventilated. It is also important that the training rooms be located to provide quiet and uninterrupted learning activity.

Equipment such as chalkboards, projectors, mockups, pictures and other audio-visual devices bring training to life. A training function should not be expected to limp along without benefit of the tools necessary for the most successful completion of the training job.

Who's Responsible?

Establishing responsibility for training in a business enterprise is not a simple matter. It is rather difficult to quarrel with the idea that training should be a line responsibility. How much top management expects its line supervisors to do in training depends upon how it generally divides responsibility for its other personnel functions. Most line supervisors jealously guard their prerogatives and have little or no desire to relinquish any part of their responsibility. They claim that *they* must accomplish the total job of subordinate development. The unfortunate fact is that training is only a part of the whole job of supervision and that employees need development on a continuous basis. Employee development, therefore, by line supervision in a formal organized manner is neglected. The most common excuse is that they do not have enough time to train every employee and perform their other supervisory duties. In an environment such as this, a new hire often feels like a fifth wheel and begins to develop frustration and fear.

If training can be thought of as a staff function, then the responsibility of personnel development can be delegated. This type of responsibility determination can be accomplished by an upper management edict.

The concept of the training department operating as a staff function with no power beyond weak and apologetic advice is a poor one indeed. If top management expects results from the training department, it must give responsibility accompanied by authority. This authority must include planning, controlling, coordinating, and administering of all education and training activities.

Where on the Organization Chart?

The training program is generally placed under the personnel director or the industrial relations director who consults with a committee of operating executives. When a training program is organized, a director should be appointed to carry out its activities and to work with a training staff in developing methods of teaching and courses that fit company needs.

Establishing the location for the authority and the responsibility for the initiation and control of employee development programs can cover a broad spectrum. In some instances it has been felt that employee development is the exclusive domain of an officially designated training department. Under these conditions, line management has had little or no part in the training program beyond releasing their employees to the training department for instruction. At the opposite end of the continuum are those companies in which there is no training administrator and it is assumed that each level of management will handle its own development of personnel.

These extremes are ineffective. If employee development is to be fully effective, then the training effort must be the joint activity and responsibility of a training administrator and the various members of supervision. In this scheme, the training director is more of a consultant—serving as adviser, coordinator, and controller. Although line management must take an active part in the determination of training within his own section, and must be prepared to carry part of the instructional load himself, it is imperative to the success of the training activities that some person within the company be designated as the responsible head of all training programs.

Training is a service department. Although much controversy occurs over where such a function should report, traditionally training reports to a personnel or industrial relations function. If we buy the idea that training is strictly a service organization, maybe we should break with tradition.

The major consideration for organizational placement must be that the training organization be placed in a function that handles activities similar to those of training and has similar objectives. This concept emphasizes that when activities that have common objectives are grouped together under one administrator, maximum utilization of available resources is attained.

A second consideration for placement is that training should be organizationally placed where it can serve ALL units of the enterprise: production, service, sales, office, legal, research, traffic, quality control, finance, etc. If the training function is centered in any one of these areas, it may be inclined to devote more attention there and "find" it difficult to serve the other units.

Regardless of his placement on the organization chart, the training director must be a member of the top echelon. Top management must recognize the fact that he is dealing with matters of vital importance to the company. Too often the training director is outside the *in group.* A training director cannot plan training to meet a need known only to the top echelon of a company's management. A training director who is a member of this upper echelon is the exception rather than the rule.

Important Steps for the Person in Charge

Once the training function is formally established, there are some important actions that should take place by the training administrator before beginning the routine of classwork.

First, and most important, is the development of close personal relationships with as many members of the management team as possible. While rubbing elbows with the top brass is fulfilling to the ego, do not neglect line management. To increase the probability that management will accept his ideas and counsel, the training administrator should strive to become known and liked throughout the business enterprise. It is an established fact of practical leadership that in listening to an individual and/or judging him, people usually will allow themselves to be influenced as much by their subjective reaction to him as a person as by the logic of his spoken ideas. Therefore, even after top management has made a yeoman effort to get acceptance of the training program, the training director must sell himself. If he does not, he is very likely to fail.

Secondly, the training staff, administrator included, must become thoroughly acquainted with all phases of the business of the company. This step is combined easily with the effort of becoming personally acquainted with the various levels of management.

A good technique is for the training director to tell the supervisors and managers that before he can determine training needs, he must be trained himself in what *their* business is about. Thus, their first contact with him is one in which they have the role of teacher, and the training director has that of the learner.

Finally, and the most often overlooked, is the development of an understanding of the processes, practices and individuals of the company. The entire training staff must know both the formal and informal organization structure. There is nothing more deadly to a training function than the formal paperwork drudgery of official channels because the informal organization structure feels slighted or left out.

The training director must study his company, both its formal and its informal structure, and he must use them both.

Otherwise his programs will bog down and he may not understand why.

Fire Fighters or Fire Preventionists?

Generally, training departments are not given the responsibility for preparing employees on a long term basis. This is the major cause for the difficulty of keeping workers abreast of new developments. When employees (new hires or old timers) are found to be lacking in ability, *then* the training department is called upon to design a program to remedy the *specific* work deficiency. These after-the-fact training programs are of necessity put together hurriedly. While such programs do not accomplish very much, it seems typical to find a training specialist donning a fireman's hat and going out to stomp out isolated brush fires.

What is necessary is a change in thinking, not only by the training director (the fire chief) but also by his boss (top management). In an effort to bring training plans in line with present and future requirements, Bienvenu[3] suggests:

1. Responsibility and authority for training must be delineated. More, its role must be defined and strengthened in order that its objectives and purposes may be in accord with the needs of the organization and its functions clearly understood.
2. The long-term plans of the organization should be broken down to the point where their effect on training can be determined. The objective is to arrive at a type of training program which will insure the existence of a work force readily able to adapt to changing demands and implement the established plans. This requires the following kind of analysis:

a. What are the plans for the future?

b. What worker qualifications will these plans require, and how many of what type of employees will be needed?

c. What is the ability and knowledge status of the existing work force in relation to future requirements?

d. What kind of plans will be required to provide the employees with the desired knowledge and skills so that they can readily adapt to new demands with minimum retraining; and can hurried, single-purpose courses be avoided?

3. The findings of this kind of analysis should be used to develop training plans in keeping with the concepts of continuous and total training.

The acceptance of the usefulness of long-range training plans must be a part of the thinking of every level of management. Without commitment to change at the top, the organization as a whole cannot move in the direction of innovation even though there may be islands of innovations: subunits of the organization, moving toward innovation to the extent that they can.[4]

Promotion Policy

Closely associated with any discussion of the establishment of training programs is the question of promotion. The trend toward sound management through effective employee relations implies that promotion is best made from within an organization. An enterprise should offer whatever help it can to its employees so that they may be ready for higher positions. One of the best aids for promotions is a formalized training program. Training courses should not be intended only for help in gaining promotion but also for the improvement of the work in the present job.

SUMMARY

To maximize the benefits of training, there has to be sound planning. The planning for the training function involves many considerations. Among the more influential are the complexity of the social economy; the pace of the changing technology; and the nature of company operations, planning and staffing. For the most beneficial results, proper planning must take place prior to the implementation of the training program. When training enjoys prestige throughout the company, then uniform knowledge and skills are presented, time required for planning training programs is lessened, scheduling is more efficient, and attendance is at its peak.

If planning for the continuous development of personnel is deemed important, then the training director must be a member of the top echelon. Giving the training function a place of significance in the enterprise will demonstrate that the top executives have a sincere interest in personnel and organization development.

If a company is to attain its organizational objectives, it must have a well-trained work force. The employee training division can aid in this attainment. If training is accepted with the same confidence as are other staff functions, such as engineering, legal, sales and service, and quality control, then a healthy relationship will be maintained. A recognition that the training division is just as concerned with company success as any other division will do much toward the achievement of a healthy relationship. To maximize this relationship, there is certain groundwork which must be done by top management prior to the formal establishment of a training department. All management personnel must be shown how the new function can help them in their work.

Formalized training programs of any kind are better than haphazard training. A company's training effort must be integrated with all the rest of its effort. Training must be given the same attention as the other major business functions if the company is to achieve optimum success and maintain its competitive position.

Actually, training organizations differ from company to company. This difference is based partly on the needs within the individual company. The most frequent approach to the organization problem is to place the training director under the supervision of the head of the personnel activity in the company concerned. But, the *most* important aspect of training division organization that must be considered is its status in relation to other staff and service activities of the business.

It must be kept in mind that the function of the training director is to promote the integration of training activities so that a given program can be accomplished efficiently and economically. To his list of functions can be added the important courses (subject matter) through which company functions (objectives) can be achieved. Courses in company history, organization, policy, and services help considerably in the orientation of new hires and supervisors. Training in principles of organization, planning, staffing, controlling, cost control and job evaluation help to develop management skills. Training in the skills and information required to perform the job will help to develop the worker's technical proficiency.

In accomplishment of the foregoing, it is important that the training department personnel make every effort to sell themselves as persons to management as well as the workers before beginning the formal training program. They should also make an intensive preliminary study of their industry or business in all its phases.

REFERENCES

1. Denova, Charles C. "Building Employee Self-Confidence on the Job: An Unexpected Benefit of Industrial Training." *Educational Technology, Training Technology Supplement,* September, 1969, pp. 29-31.

2. Denova, Charles C. "Is This Any Way to Evaluate a Training Program? You Bet It Is!" *Personnel Journal,* July, 1968, pp. 488-493.

3. Bienvenu, Bernard J. *New Priorities in Training.* New York: American Management Association, Inc., 1969.

4. Schon, Donald A. *Technology and Change.* New York: Delacorte Press, 1967.

2.

Establishing the Conditions for Learning

Training is conducted to develop two things, a pattern of thinking and a pattern of acting. It is the job of the instructor to insure that his trainees are properly motivated to take the necessary action required to perceive those things that they should

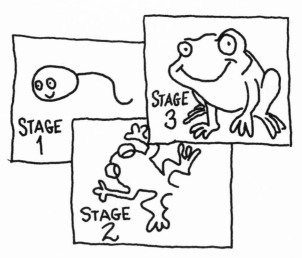

DEVELOPMENTAL APPROACH

learn. Action by the trainee is necessary before the reception of a stimulus becomes learning. One cannot sit back and learn. Learning is an active process; it implies a change in behavior. The instructor is charged with the responsibility to cause the change for development.

INDIVIDUAL DIFFERENCES

Perhaps the most challenging thing about teaching is that there are no two individuals exactly alike, and no two classes exactly alike. Learners differ from one another in looks, interests, abilities, likes and dislikes, understanding, and rate of learning. Therefore, in planning learning activities that provide the optimum of motivation, the instructor needs to recognize that individual differences stand out as a critical factor.

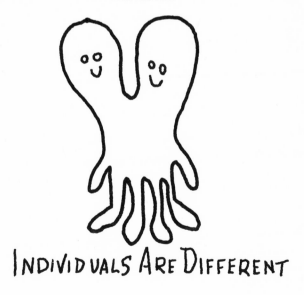

INDIVIDUALS ARE DIFFERENT

Individual learners vary in their reactions. The instructor must study each member of his class so that his instructions will secure favorable reaction from the greatest number—all of them, if possible. The greatest single factor in lesson/course consideration is that individual differences must be recognized. Instructors have not always recognized this factor or have been unable to develop a concept to cope with it. The important thing is to keep trying. Arnold Hagen [1] states, "We frankly admit that teaching is an art, much more than it is a science, largely learned in the crucible of experience, and refined through trial and error in the classroom."

PSYCHOLOGY OF LEARNING

The needs, attitudes and capabilities of learners are not only different but also of fundamental importance to the instructor. To ignore them is to provide a classroom experience that will be certain to result in indifference by the learner and lead to frustration on the part of the instructor. To implement learning, good teaching is required. Good teaching is based on a reasonable understanding of how individuals learn. Mort and Vincent [2] have developed and compiled one of the most complete references on the psychology of learning and teaching. Their guides of value to trainers are contained in this basic listing:

1. *No one learns without feeling some urge to learn.* It may be fear, need, inborn drive, curiosity, mystery, challenge, importance, or personal attachment—or any other motivating force. The force has to be there, and the more the force swells up out of the person himself, the more the person will learn of his own accord.

2. *What a person learns is influenced directly by his surroundings.* If you want a person to learn something, make that

thing a part of his environment so that he may see it, live with it, be influenced by it.

3. *A person learns most quickly and lastingly what has meaning for him.* The learner does not always see the meanings the instructor sees. An act takes on meaning from its outcome—what the act produces. To produce a thing he wants or can see the value of, a person is likely to master the skill necessary.

4. *When an organism is ready to act, it is painful for it not to act; and when an organism is not ready to act, it is painful for it to act.* This means that some time must be spent in preparing learners to learn, that physical action is as much a part of school as mental action.

5. *Individuals differ in all sorts of ways.* When you get a group of people together to do anything, some will be better than others. It is easy to see that some people are taller than others, less easy to see that in dozens of abilities that relate to success in learning any class will show a vast range of differences.

6. *Security and success are the soil and climate for growth.* No one can learn well when he doesn't belong—any more than a plant can grow without roots in the soil. No one can succeed on failure.

7. *All learning occurs through attempts to satisfy needs.* What people do, consciously or not, they do because of need; and as they do, they learn what to do to satisfy need.

8. *Emotional tension decreases efficiency in learning.* Before the skills and facts of teaching come friendliness, security, acceptance, and belief in success. Without these, tensions are procured. Constant, monotonous attention to any one thing is also a producer of tension.

9. *Physical defects lower efficiency in learning.* A sound

mind in a sound body. For greatest efficiency in any kind of teaching, physical health comes before mental vigor.

10. *Interest is an indicator of growth.* We don't teach to get interest, but if interest isn't present, the teaching isn't prospering.

11. *Interest is a source of power in motivating learning.* When you are interested in a thing, you are in it and feel a part of it. An instructor who doesn't hook his teaching to whatever learners feel they are already a part of is not making the greatest use of the powers he has at his command.

12. *What gives satisfaction tends to be repeated; what is annoying tends to be avoided.* Practice makes perfect only when it is the right kind of practice. Learning is efficient if the student tries to master what fits his abilities and gives satisfaction.

13. *The best way to learn a part in life is to play that part.* This is the apprenticeship idea. Upon leaving the classroom, the parts in life which learners play are not completely new to them if they have practiced those parts in class.

14. *Learning is more efficient and longer lasting when the conditions for it are real and lifelike.* Attitudes, habits and skills for life are best learned when the activities of school are like those of life. Methods of teaching should be as much as possible like those one uses in actual living.

15. *Piecemeal learning is not efficient.* We learn facts and skills best when we learn them in a pattern, not as isolated bits of subject matter. The facts and skills that we learn become part of a pattern when we learn them in relation to their use—as part of a project, job, or other enterprise.

16. *You can't train the mind like a muscle.* There is no body of knowledge that is the key to "mind-training." There is no set of exercises that will "sharpen the wits" as a grindstone will sharpen steel. This means: don't isolate the things you want to teach from the real setting in which they belong.

17. *A person learns by his own activity.* He learns what he does; he gains insight as he learns to organize what he does. Within certain limits, the more extensive a learner's activity, the greater will be his learning.

18. *Abundant, realistic practice contributes to learning.* Learners need much practice in the many intellectual, creative and social acts which we want them to master.

19. *Participation enhances learning.* Participation is essential to any complex learning. Complete participation is important—from planning to checking results.

20. *Firsthand experience makes for lasting and more complete learning.* Learners need experience between reading and hearing about something secondhand and the kind of knowledge and insight that come from firsthand experience.

21. *General behavior is controlled by emotions as well as by intellect.* The modern instructor is concerned with training the emotions as well as the mind.

22. *Unused talents contribute to personal maladjustment.* Not only are unused talents a waste to society; they form a core of dissatisfaction to the individual. Frustrated talent can lead to many kinds of neurotic symptoms.

23. *You start to grow from where you are and not from some artificial starting point.* It is unrealistic to assume that pupils can move through the grades of school like taking the steps on a ladder jumping from step to step. It is impossible to move a pupil on

from some point or grade standard that he has not yet achieved.

24. *Growth is a steady, continuous process, and different individuals grow at different rates.* It is impossible for a class of first-graders to move along all together. Each individual learns, but at his own rate.

25. *It is impossible to learn one thing at a time.* It is impossible to turn everything else off while learning "two times two." The learner as a whole responds to his setting as a whole and takes in many things besides "two times two." Learning by problems, topics and projects, replacing learning by bits, makes capital of this fact.

26. *Learning is reinforced when two or more senses are used at the same time.* One-cylinder learning sticks only to reading or only to listening. Students learn better if they see with the eyes, touch with the hands, hear with the ears, heft with the muscles, at the same time they are "seeing" with the mind.

27. *The average learner is largely a myth.* Standards are an average which every learner is expected to achieve. But any standard that you can set will be too difficult for some, too easy for others. The achievement of a group scatters over a wide range—only a few are at the "average" point. A far greater number are scattered above and below the average.

28. *If you want a certain result, teach it directly.* Your students are not born with the skills you want them to have; nor can we always depend upon others to teach to our satisfaction. If your students do not know what you want them to know, the most efficient thing to do is to teach it to them.

29. *Learners develop in terms of all the influences which affect them.* Not only the days at work but the 365 days of living at home and in the community go into making a person what he becomes.

According to Mort and Vincent, these guides can be used in a number of ways: to judge the *variety* of the instructor's practice, to judge the psychological *validity* of his practice, to *test* new practices, and to *justify* his practice.

PRACTICE OF A SKILL

A major concern should be in providing the best atmosphere for the proper application of practice, the doing of the skill or the application of the knowledge. Adequate opportunity for practice is essential in learning a skill, but, because of their repetitious nature, many drill activities become monotonous and thereby decrease in their educational value.

Practice should be conducted under conditions similar to those which will exist during the use of the skill, and the procedures practiced must be those in which the skill is desired.

Denova[3] found that practice on training aids and scrap parts interfered with the maximum development of trainee self-confidence during vestibule training. He found that seventy-three percent of the trainees spent much of their time checking and rechecking before they performed the same tasks and operations they had practiced many times in the classroom without hesitation. "You see, we were now working for real," was the explanation.

In providing drill for students of typewriting, an older method called for a great amount of drill on nonsense syllables.[4] It was thought that since these movements were used extensively in actual typewriting, the dexterity acquired in this would be readily transferred to the writing situation in which they would be used. Since modern educational technology has found that one learns more effectively and more efficiently what one practices, modern typewriting methods call for the student to start practice on sentences as soon as the keyboard is learned.

ABILITY TO DEVELOP

There are several activities through which individuals learn. The selection of the activities depends on what is to be accomplished. The selected activity should make the principle, idea, or skill more graphic, more interesting. We learn what we practice. It seems that if we practice nonsense, we learn nonsense; if we practice on scrap, we learn to produce scrap. The alternative seems obvious.

THE WHOLE VS. THE PART

Learning is a combination of a number of factors which can be referred to as *"the whole."* Those who hold that the whole is most important are part of the Gestalt school of psychology. They feel that learning comes best from analyzing the whole rather than attempting to add parts to make it a unified pattern. In other words, *the whole is more than the sum of its parts.*

Many leading education psychologists tend to suggest the Gestalt approach, but Symonds[5] reports that although the whole-method of teaching is superior in many respects to other instructional patterns, caution by the instructor should be exercised in using the method:

1. The whole-method has proved itself to be superior in memorizing.
2. The whole-method becomes less efficient when the passage to be memorized becomes too long or difficult.
3. The whole-method becomes increasingly effective with increasing practice in using the method.
4. The whole-method, or a progressive part-method, leads to superior learning of acts of skill.
5. With material of a given level of difficulty, the mentally more mature individual can profit more from learning by a whole-method.
6. The whole-method is superior when there is a distribution of learning over several practice periods.
7. One should consider wholeness not in terms of the totality of what is to be learned, but in terms of the degree of integration of the unit to be learned.
8. Learning is most efficient when one first grasps the

meaning and organization of the whole, and then proceeds to give attention to the parts and the relation of each part to the other parts and to the whole.

9. Learning is more efficient when the material to be learned is meaningful and rich in associations.

10. One should attempt to learn only that which he understands and comprehends. If material to be learned is beyond the comprehension of the learner, it should be simplified or broken down into meaningful parts.

THE CONDITIONS FOR LEARNING

If training is to be effective, the conditions of learning must be favorable in the following three areas:

1. Curiosity must be aroused,
2. Appropriate information provided, and
3. Satisfying practice conditions made possible.

It is the responsibility of the instructor to bring tangible results to the trainees in each of the three areas mentioned above.

Arousing Curiosity

The ability of human beings to absorb and use knowledge is in itself no reason for doing so. Intelligence alone does not assure the acquisition of knowledge. What then is the key? The necessary element is to arouse curiosity—MOTIVATION. In establishing favorable conditions for learning, arousing curiosity is synonymous with motivation.

The instructor must motivate the trainee to do. Therefore, the aims of the program must be clearly recognized, because

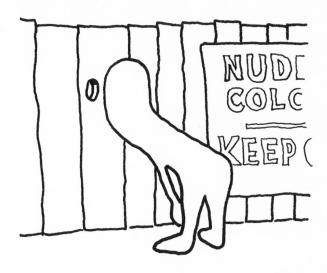

motives which are significant in the learning process include interest, attitudes, needs and purposes. Learning is most efficient when the activities to be performed are the means of satisfying the trainee's needs or assisting him in attaining important goals.

If desirable conduct is to follow from the instruction that is a change in behavior, which is often called learning, the instruction must be ego satisfying. This means that interests and drives of the learners must be recognized and used to advantage through emphasis on the most appropriate teaching devices and teaching methods. The instructor must use incentives, most often subtly, sometimes dramatically, but he must use them if curiosity is to be aroused for positive behavioral changes.

Appropriate Information
In teaching, the instructor tries to organize learning experiences so that the learning of the first task facilitates the learning in

a second learning experience, and so forth. He also provides learning experiences in the classroom that are appropriate enough to transfer to the out-of-classroom situations, e.g., to the job environment. In the final analysis, a training program can best be justified *only* if it can be shown that classroom learning has beneficial effects on the out-of-classroom behavior of the learner.

The following is McGeoch and Irion's[6] explanation of how transfer occurs:

> Transfer of training occurs whenever the existence of a previously established habit has an influence upon the acquisition, performance, or relearning of a second habit. It is one of the most general phenomena of learning and, by means of its influence, almost all learned behavior is inter-related in various complex ways. Transfer serves to determine, in part, the ease of learning of a particular habit, and indeed, every new learning takes place in the context of all previously established habits.

Depending on the appropriateness of the information or tasks performed, transfer may be positive or negative. Positive transfer occurs when the learning of one task facilitates the learning or performance of the second task. Negative transfer occurs when the learning of the first task interferes with the learning of performance of the second task.

To a considerable extent, providing appropriate information and practice insures positive transfer of learning to the real job environment. The similarity of relationships between two learning situations affects transfer and retention. Retention and positive transfer are more likely to occur when the responses to be learned in two tasks are functionally identical.

Importance of Success

To be successful, the learner must experience a feeling of accomplishment. It is the responsibility of the instructor to see to it that his trainees do succeed. We learn by our successes. Success is said to breed success, and failure to breed failure.

Some differences in performance of trainees may be attributable to differences in achievement motivation. People with a strong need to achieve are motivated when they perceive a task as important, while individuals of low need-achievement are motivated more by intrinsic rewards.

Success and failure affect motivation. Each group of trainees builds a system of norms. That is to say, they establish ways in which *they* expect other members of the group to behave. These norms influence an individual's performance. To understand the motivation of employees, it is helpful to understand the environmental pressures of the company, job and/or trainee peer group.

REFERENCES

1. Hagen, Arnold J. "S-R Bonds," *Phi Delta Kappan,* June, 1959, p. 389.

2. Mort, Paul R. & William S. Vincent. *Introduction to American Education.* New York: McGraw-Hill Book Company, Inc., 1954.

3. Denova, Charles C. *An Assessment of the Effect on Self-Confidence of the Acquisition of New Skills.* Unpublished dissertation for Doctorate from U.C.L.A., 1968.

4. Kingsley, Howard L. & Ralph Garry. *The Nature and Conditions of Learning.* Englewood Cliffs, New Jersey: Prentice-Hall, Inc., 1957.

5.   Symonds, Percival M. "What Education Has to Learn from Psychology." *Teachers College Record,* March, 1957, pp. 332-333.

6.   McGeoch, J.A. & A.L. Irion. *The Psychology of Human Learning.* New York: David McKay Company, Inc., 1952.

3.
Techniques in Developing Training Programs

One need not be a prophet to predict the one thing that is certain for the future—CHANGE. There will be a constant change in information and technology. Constant changes in occupational life result in a need for constant changes in training procedures and programs. New courses constantly must be devised to meet changed job situations. When training is given without adequate planning based upon actual company needs, it is likely to be ineffective. In the period ahead, further occupational changes will take place, resulting in even more adjustment in job-training materials and programs. If a training program is to be given for a half-dozen workers, and if the training need be given only once, program designers obviously are not justified in giving the same amount of attention to course development that would be justified if this training were to be given to several thousand trainees. If a course is to be used for several years, almost any amount of time given to course planning that will produce better results is justified.

In the procedures suggested in this discussion, modifications will always be necessary to meet individual cases—eliminating many of the details suggested, or sometimes elaborating on them. The general structure, nevertheless, will serve as a guide in planning any course of study—skill development and management development. In view of the trying circumstances under which most training administrators work, however, the ill-fitted and specialized training that they have received, and the heavy administrative loads, well-defined training programs are the *sine qua non* of a good system.

The training program should not shackle the progressive training director; rather it should aid him to execute his task more efficiently. The ideal program should help the trainee learn to do better those desirable job activities that he will do anyway. In the preparation of training programs, therefore, actual needs and activities of trainees should be given first consideration; and the beliefs of educational theorists should be secondary.

One thing is certain, change will come, whether planned or not. But a piecemeal approach will no longer provide the kinds of solutions training programs need today. There must be a clear idea of the ultimate outcome of all training programs.

A CURRICULUM VS. A COURSE

A curriculum and a course of study must be differentiated. A course of study is a selection of topics closely grouped around a major interest. It is synonymous with "subject." Labor law, for example, is a course of study. A curriculum is a series of courses whose goal is the attainment by the learner of a high standard of development in the broadest sense of the word. Naturally, the first step in selecting subject matter is to determine the educational efficiency that is to serve as the curricular goal.

The selection of subject matter involves two major processes: 1) the selection of subject matter for individual courses, and 2) the development of a curriculum out of a series of courses. In most respects, curriculum construction is only an extension of course making. Supervisor development is an example of a curriculum.

SUBJECT MATTER SELECTION

There are two general ways in which subject matter can be selected—subjectively and objectively. The distinction between the two methods is not absolute and in the final analysis is purely a matter of degree.

In seeking a starting point from which to make the selection of subject matter, there also appear to be two groups, marked by divergent attitudes. One group, the subjectivists, would begin with subject matter and build upon it. The other group, the objectivists, would start *de novo*. The latter tend to ignore the present program as completely as possible and start fresh. Another characteristic of the objectivists is that they believe that the learner is king and not the subject matter. Here again the distinction is relative rather than absolute.

The Subjective Method. In the subjective method, the training-program designer marshals his prejudices and personal experiences and then goes to work. He generally analyzes existing courses in an effort to determine what is wrong with them. Thus he "corrects" weaknesses in accordance with his ideas of how trainees should learn. Whether or not they really learn as he thinks they should is irrelevant.

Sometimes the subjectivist recognizes that other educators whose opinions count must be consulted. The compounded wisdom of a committee of experts, he feels, cannot be wrong. This procedure has been called (by its opponents, of course) "the method of collective ignorance." Adversaries of the method say that the pooling of much ignorance does not create less ignorance, but more.

Sometimes the subjective designer attempts to give an objective cast to his program by undertaking a survey of existing training programs, in order to find out what is being taught. An analysis, in terms of frequency, of the surveyed material is often the basis of many training classes, a procedure that assumes that the average is right. In practice, the survey method tends to continue existing curricular weaknesses. There is no evidence that courses formed in this way meet the demands of the business enterprise better than those upon which they are based.

Need for Subjective Selection of Subject Matter. The "scissors and paste" method, for all its subjectivity, is useful and necessary within its limitations. In fact, the only way in which the ultimate objectives of training can be determined is on a basis of subjective judgment. The purposes of training are, in the final analysis, a matter of top management's opinion; and, therefore, the core about which all training activities revolve must be subjective. Only the details can be determined objectively.

In no case is it possible to remove completely the subjective element from curriculum materials. In many instances, the so-called objective method is merely an impersonal way of choosing personal opinions.

The Objective Method. In the objective method of subject matter selection, no references are made to existing subject matter. Significant elements are determined objectively. By this means, the formalism of the old course material is avoided; the new course is freed as far as possible from previous prejudices and can, therefore, approximate more closely the actual needs of *the company*—a good synonym for trainees. Although in the past the subjective method has been used rather exclusively, the more progressive training directors now tend to adhere to objective procedures.

THE ANSWERS AID DECISION-MAKING

In the process of course decision-making, these eleven questions must be answered:

1. What is the justification for the training of *that* position?
2. What information, skills, or attitudes are to be changed?
3. How extensive should training be? To an acquaintance-ship or a mastership level?
4. Where should training take place? On the job, in the classroom or off-site?
5. When? On company time, before or after hours, or a combination?
6. How should the information be presented? In what sequence, and with what instructional methods?
7. Who shall teach? The job supervisor, the training department specialist, or both?
8. Who are the participants? Men, women, or both? What is their ability level?
9. How long shall the training be? One hour, one day, one week, or one month?

10. What equipment, facilities, manuals, and materials are needed? How many of each?
11. How should the participants, the program, and the instructional techniques be evaluated?

Why give the training? The justification of any training course must be determined in terms of job value. Do the workers need to be trained for this purpose? If so, is the training better given formally or informally? Should it be presented by the job supervisor, the training department, or some outside agency? Should the trainees be taught on company time, during, after, and/or before regular working hours, or in some combination?

What should be taught? This is based to a large degree on why and what particular ability or skill is needed. This, plus the trainee's level of ability, gives the general pattern. The training details must be based on an actual research analysis of the job needs. This involves job analysis. It is important that training course designers be familiar with job analysis techniques so as to include the important teaching elements, the key points, and activities related to the job. This analysis is a *must* since it will determine the number of duties performed and the frequency of their occurrence. This type of job information is not adequately found elsewhere.

How well should "they" be taught? How well each job should be learned depends on a number of factors. If the employee needs little training in order to make use of a skill on the job and can then develop mastership there, then a familiarization is sufficient. There are cases when the employee is useless unless he has developed mastership previous to job use. This can only be determined from a study of the job under consideration for training.

Where and with what equipment should the course be taught? Where a course is to be taught requires an analysis of the available space. It is also determined, in part, by a decision on where the skill or knowledge is to be learned—on or off the job. Individuals who design courses do not necessarily control space allocations, so this factor is a major consideration. Space decisions are influenced by what equipment and materials are to be used. With what equipment and facilities the course is taught depends on the job needs as well as the materials available. Will the trainee use the equipment? Are special training devices needed to facilitate learning? A major concern of management is: To what extent will learning on operational facilities and equipment interfere with business operations?

What should be the course sequence? Once course content has been established, then consideration can be given to sequence. Course sequence depends upon many factors. Content is a major influence. The trainee is another. The instructor may be considered the most influential of all factors.

What teaching method shall be used? The manner in which the materials shall be presented to the learner must be carefully determined. Sometimes the straight lecture is adequate; other times, the lecture-demonstration; at still other times, the work-sheet procedure is most desirable. Selection of teaching method depends on several factors, some of which are instructional purposes, time limits, materials to be used, degree of thoroughness, facilities, budget restrictions, instructor, and most of all—*the trainee.*

The modern instructor has numerous instructional techniques from which to choose. An instructional method that is effective for one type of training objective (e.g., changing supervisors' attitudes toward merit reviews) may not be effective for another type of training objective (e.g., imparting information on company policies). Therefore, the kind of change in learner behavior that the instructor is attempting to effect must be kept in mind when selecting learning activities. Choosing appropriate instructional techniques involves selecting tasks that are meaningful at an appropriate level of difficulty for the learner.

Who shall instruct? This is a question that is greatly influenced by philosophy—top management, or the training director? Some companies feel that only training specialists are qualified to give the training. There are others that believe a competent worker can do the training. If a competent worker is to be a trainer, provision should be made for giving him detailed aid in working out the teaching procedures. On the other hand, if a training specialist is to give the training, there must be an assurance that he has full opportunity to learn the work and that he has made use of his opportunities.

How long should training be? There can be only one answer: Until the trainee has achieved the desired level of skill. This is why it is so important to *first* determine how well the employee will be taught—to an acquaintanceship or to a mastership level. The question of length should be part of the final phase of any particular training design. Most of the other course related decisions should be made first.

When should training be conducted? Training must be conducted when needed, and should not be conducted when it cannot be economically justified. Also, part of the *when* question is where to start—at what level? There is no single best place to start training; let it begin wherever there is a need for it, there is recognition of that need, there is enthusiasm among those who need it, and there is a training program that can be made available to meet the need.

Is evaluation necessary? Evaluation *is* necessary in order to be able to report on the effectiveness of the training program. A follow-up of the learners to determine how effectively they are using their training on the job is a must. It serves as a means of improving instruction and uncovers the need for remedial training.

The planning process is not complete without a specific plan for evaluation. Program evaluation is a process of determining the extent to which specific objectives and predetermined levels of skills were attained. Management uses evaluation to insure that intentions are actually realized and that desired effects are achieved.

To determine if the best, most economical training program was conducted, a diagnostic study of every aspect of training is a must. An effective evaluation plan covers these major aspects:

1. The assessment of the change in employee behavior.
2. An analysis of whether or not the training furthers the attainment of organizational goals.
3. An evaluation of the training personnel, methods, and techniques.

Evaluation is not an easy task, but it must be done and done completely.

SUMMARY

Continuous planning and decision-making should make course designers better planners and better guessers. Piet Hein expressed it well when he stated:

> Err
> and err
> and err again
> but less
> and less
> and less.*

Comprehensive training program planning is the application of the systems approach. It does not deal with each separate element alone, but permits the course designer to see things as part of a whole. This type of planning permits every level of management to focus on the major issues relevant to the successful survival of the company.

In contrast to this type of approach is the *ad hoc* informal approach to planning which takes place only when a problem arises. This approach is random and has shortcomings. Mainly, it generally results in decisions which narrow choices available for future action and, therefore, is costly.

*Hein, Piet. "The Road to Wisdom," *Life,* October 14, 1966.

4.

Job Analysis: The Best Procedure for Course Design

It is impossible to recommend a course that would be equally good for every company, because there are too many special features in each organization to which the training program must be adapted. The most essential step in the development of a successful training program or even a single course is the establishment of detailed and accurate training needs. Many training needs are not obvious without a searching analysis.

THREE PRONG ANALYSIS

In order to determine the organizational development requirements, an analysis must be made in three major areas:

Area one	—	Organizational Analysis
Area two	—	Operations Analysis
Area three	—	Man Analysis

Organizational Analysis. Before training personnel can determine future training needs, they must have a clear picture of the present organization structure and desirable future changes based on projected expansions, acquisitions or mergers, as well as on new products or functions which may develop. An organization chart of the present positions and responsibilities is therefore a must. Also, top management's thinking might be projected ahead into what an organizational chart of the future may look like in order to serve as a guide to make possible improvements either in operations or in personnel.

The analysis of present and future organizational structure raises questions such as the following:*

1.   Are some responsibilities assigned to certain positions because of special capacities or deficiencies of individuals now occupying those positions? Should these positions be realigned if these men were transferred, promoted, or retired?

2.   Are all the present positions necessary, or can responsibilities be regrouped for more effective operations now?

3.   Is each position so organized that the individual holding it knows what is expected of him? Has he participated in setting his objectives? Does he know what his responsibilities are?

4.   Would a different grouping of responsibilities be more effective if the organization should grow in size during the next five or ten years? For example, some companies have changed from functional divisions such as manufacturing, sales, research, engineering, etc., to product divisions, with each of these functions coordinated by the division manager to achieve maximum profit for the product division. Would this type of

*Pigors, Paul and Charles A. Meyers. *Personnel Administration: A Point of View and A Method.* New York: McGraw-Hill Book Company, 1965.

organizational structure be more effective in developing all-round executives?

5.   Do staff people have so much responsibility for procedures and methods that line managers no longer feel responsible for results and tend to "pass the buck" to the staff?

Answers to these questions need to be based upon an analysis of present positions and the qualifications of the individuals needed to fill them. This organizational analysis approach to determine employee developmental requirements emphasizes the need of the training administrator to be a member of the top echelon in order that he may have easy access to the foregoing information.

Operations Analysis. An analysis of the present and future organizational structures makes it possible to determine the need for development and/or replacement. The analysis will determine what should be the contents of the development training in terms of what the employees must do to perform the task, the job, or the assignment in the most effective way. This analysis must be done for the future jobs and tasks as well as those of the present.

All this requires advance manpower planning. This type of analysis also requires a manpower audit and a replacement chart or table. These are necessary in order to have a convenient way of summarizing the kinds of operations that will exist. Indeed, this approach assumes that top management always knows best about the future development of its subordinate employees. True or not, it is the management philosophy most training administrators must live with.

Man Analysis. Before doing the analysis of the man, two points are important: first, it is important to have a clear-cut understanding regarding the exact demands of the job (the technical content of the job being in conformity to what is stated in the job description), and second, that the need is definite and realistic regarding what supervision wants.

However efficient recruitment procedures are, not all candidates will prove acceptable as regular workers. (This is the main reason for establishing a training function.) Every new employee, regardless of his previous training, education and experience, needs to be introduced to the work environment of his new employer and to be taught how to perform specific tasks. Therefore, an analysis of the man is necessary to determine what skills, knowledge and attitudes must be developed if he is to perform the tasks which constitute his job in the organization.

PROCEDURE IN COURSE DESIGNING

The course designer must first determine the elements that go into a course. The most tangible procedure is that of the job analysis. One of the most quoted definitions of "job analysis" is as follows:*

> *Job Analysis* is defined as the process of determining, by observation and study, and reporting pertinent information relating to the nature of a specific job. It is the determination of the tasks which comprise the job and of the skills, knowledges, abilities and responsibilities required of the worker for successful performance and which differentiate the job from all others.

*U.S. Employment Service, Occupational Analysis and Industrial Services Division. *Training and Reference Manual for Job Analysis,* June, 1944.

For the purpose of personnel administration, job facts are collected through job analysis for many reasons—job evaluation, merit rating, selection and placement, safety, and elimination of overlapping duties to mention just a few. For training purposes, job facts are secured through job analysis to provide detailed information about what the worker is to do in performing his job. This analysis becomes the core of determining the must-know items in the course content. Accurate evaluation or measurement of performance can be achieved only if it is based on accurate and complete job facts.

A word picture (the job description) is necessary to bring into focus the duties, responsibilities and organizational relationships that constitute a given job or position. The job analysis will define continuing work assignments and a scope of responsibility.

Elements Analyzed

When the job analysis is used to discover the activities of a given position in order to devise learning specifications, at least four methods may be followed: introspection, interviewing, working on the job site, and the questionnaire. Usually all these are employed in varying degrees.

The analysis may be made of:
1. Duties, job operations, or steps undertaken
2. Difficulties or errors involved in performance
3. Method of performance
4. Function of the position
5. Skills involved in performance
6. Attitudes or character traits required in the position.

Data may be obtained from one, several, or all of these job elements, at one time or separately. Attitudes and traits required in a position are frequently better analyzed separately, because they are more intangible and the learning process is different.

This book is not a manual of detailed instructions about how a job analyst should meet all the requirements of his job. For detailed information see E. Lanham, *Job Evaluation,* McGraw-Hill Book Company, New York, 1955, especially Chapter 8, "Job Analysis," pages 124-175.

Some Limitations of the Job-Analysis Technique. Many course designers do not use the job-analysis step because they need to organize their facts into training materials immediately and could not take the time required. Moreover, the procedure does not provide a learning and teaching breakdown of the steps in each job. It is strong on analysis, but weak on synthesis.

A good training procedure requires that the analyst always make some organized study of the job needs. Retrospection is helpful. It is known, however, that retrospection is always colored by an individual's wishes and previous background. Another weakness of the job analysis is that it emphasizes concrete activities. The thinking that goes on in undertaking an activity is usually ignored. Finally, a major weakness is complete failure to differentiate between duties, jobs, operations, and even steps.

The use of an occupational analysis brings up the question of transfer of training. Learning and doing are two different things. When job analysis is used as the basis for a course of study, it is assumed that the transfer of training from a learning situation to a performing situation takes place under ideal conditions.

A job analysis reveals what men actually do at work, but not what they *should* do. While training is sometimes prevented from acting as an *improver,* this function should always be its ideal. Training should not only promote the application of the best business practices, but should also delineate the nature of future improvements.

An occupational analysis presents a picture of men working at specific, and often minute, tasks. It does not synthesize seemingly unconnected segments into the unified process. The job analysis is fairly satisfactory for routine or mechanical occupations; but when the activities are primarily mental, the analysis can reveal only a fragment of the responsibility of the employee.

The job analysis presents only the occupational bases for making a course of study, although usually there are other purposes for which the course is given. In spite of its limitations, the job analysis is still the best foundation on which to construct a course of study; and, with proper refinement, many of its weaknesses may be reduced to insignificance.

SUMMARY

Job descriptions can be an asset or a liability. A job description is a liability if it is inaccurate, incomplete or out-of-date. From a training point of view, this is disadvantageous because the course designer will base his programs on false premises. This is why the course designer must visit the job site in person—to "see" for himself what is really being performed on the job.

Job descriptions can be an asset if they cover every position in the organization offering an operational view of the whole, and showing that every job in the company has been designed and analyzed as an integral part of a total effort. Such job descriptions become most valuable when they are supplemented by training.

5.

Organizing Activities for Development

Once the decision is made to teach the trainees something, several kinds of activities are necessary if the instructor is to succeed:

    a.   He must decide upon the goals he intends to reach at the end of his course of instruction.

    b.   He must select procedures, content and methods which are relevant to these goals.

    c.   He must cause the learner to interact with appropriate subject matter in accordance with principles of learning.

    d.   He must measure or evaluate the learner's performance according to the goals originally selected.

Systematic analysis provides the instructor with a structural frame work to be used as a basis for his course development. With this analysis, the instructor can select the tasks he will need to analyze in order to present them effectively. He can identify all the materials he plans to use. When he has organized these materials and decides upon the methods by which they will be employed, he will have the elements needed to develop the lesson plans for the course under development.

The success of teaching is embodied with a well-thought-out plan. There are at least these major steps:*

STEP 1: IDENTIFICATION OF THE PROGRAM

What to teach? This question plagues everyone who has an assignment to conduct training. Whatever topic is selected, it is that which the instructor hopes to impart to the learner. Subject

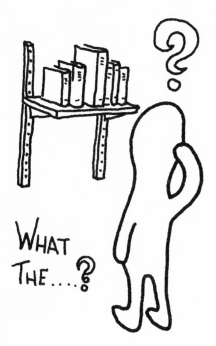

WHAT THE....?

*A similar discussion of the steps is also found in *The Executive's Guide to Training Employees in Business and Industry*. Chicago: The Dartnell Corporation, 1970.

matter selected and taught must meet the needs of the company, whether the topics are to develop knowledge, skills, or attitudes.

STEP 2: DEFINITION OF TRAINEE POPULATION

It is a good idea to write a description of the learners for whom the training is intended. The writing-out is necessary to aid the decision making that will occur during the organization of instructional material.

No matter what arguments are advanced to the contrary, the fact remains that the individuals chosen for a particular class are the ones to be trained. Whatever their shortcomings and limitations, it seems reasonable to start where *they* are. The few words of description will aid in determining where they are—knowledge-wise, that is.

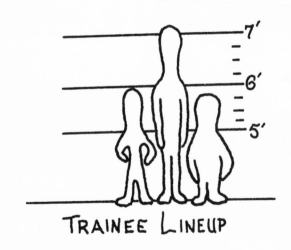

TRAINEE LINEUP

STEP 3: SPECIFICATION OF OBJECTIVES

The importance of preparing statements of objectives for each educational and/or training intent cannot be overemphasized. To be effective, it is necessary to prepare the statements of objectives in behavioral terms. The behavioral statements must specify what the learner will be doing when he is demonstrating that he is achieving specific objectives.

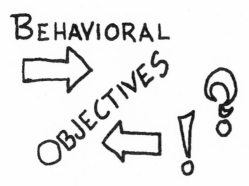

STEP 4: SPECIFICATION OF TERMINAL KNOWLEDGE

How will the instructor know when the learner has *actually* succeeded in achieving the specified objectives? It must be remembered that the interest is in demonstrating that the learner has achieved the objectives *specified.* The answer, then, is to prepare a criterion examination—a final examination.

The preparation of the final examination at this point is to prevent writing a test that measures *what happens* to be included in the lesson content rather than one that measures how well the specified objectives were achieved.

O**N**LY
W**I**TH
X-R**AY**
E**YE**S

STEP 5: DETERMINATION OF KNOWN VERSUS UNKNOWN

The exercise of preparing the criterion examination was necessary to facilitate the decisions as to what can or cannot be assumed as prior knowledge and experience on the part of the learner. These assumptions (prerequisites) must be put down on paper. Every time an assumption is made that the learner has prior knowledge of a particular process, concept, or term, it must be added to the list of prerequisites. If the decision is made that the learner is not familiar with the topic under consideration, that assumption is added to the list of things to be taught.

NOTE

 This list will be one of the most useful documents during the preparation sequence. Refer to it, add to it, and subtract from it.

STEP 6: DETERMINATION OF CONTENT

The prerequisites define where the learner is, and the objectives identify where the learner *is going.* The course content outline contains the learning opportunities that will make it possible for the learner to move from one point to the other. The criterion examination indicates when the learner has achieved the specified objectives.

Time is spent during this phase of organization in the development of a complete and accurate outline of the *content* that is intended to be transmitted to the learner.

> Do not waste time deciding on a sequence; spend your time checking that all the necessary material is in the hat (the content outline).

STEP 7: DETERMINATION OF SEQUENCE

Now that the course designer has all of the desired cards in the hat, he must stop and do some careful considering as to what will be the best sequence for THIS material for THESE learners.

To determine lesson or course sequence, the instructor must know *exactly* what he wants to teach. He must organize the points of information in a logical, easy-to-grasp progression of ideas. He must write down the points he wishes to make, jotting down notes about illustrative material, writing out quotes, and sketching his summary and review. This is the lesson outline. Yes, it is a skeleton, but it will help keep the instructor on the logical track of his preparation.

There are several strategies of sequencing the instructional material. Content may be organized according to natural or logical sequence, ease of learning, interest of the learner, need of the learner, or according to life situations, experiences, or problems. Let the subject matter, objectives, and intended learner be the important guides.

PROCEDURES IN LESSON PLANNING

The success of training is embodied with providing a situation with a maximum of motivational impetus. The instructor must anticipate the opportunities for guidance of trainees as they learn through actually performing things which we call the job. Another primary consideration for lesson planning is the conservation of lost time resulting from unguided learning activities.

Activity in a classroom does not reflect that learning is taking place; it may instead be a reflection of confusion, wasted time or lack of instructor control and direction. On the other hand, activity which follows careful instructor planning, which shows evidence of controlled trainee activity in which the trainees are working cooperatively in an orderly fashion, is a desirable situation. The latter type of classroom atmosphere does not just happen. It is the result of careful thought.

Where Are They Going?

Knowing where he is headed during each lesson gives the learner the best perspective of each activity. Also, knowing what is expected helps place the new knowledge or skill in its proper setting. In order to make the most effective approach in the solution of problem activities and/or to give his best performance of the skill, the learner must know what is expected of him and understand the reason for its accomplishment. If this is true, then, it seems reasonable that if the instructor knows where *he* is going, he must tell the learner. How else can they arrive at the same place at the same time?

When the instructor is in front of the class, he should have just one goal in mind—to communicate ideas to the learner as clearly and interestingly as possible.

Adjust the Lesson Plan, Not the Learner

Always adapt the lesson plan to the situation. During the presentation of a lesson, it may be found that the initial lesson plan sequences are not leading to the desired results. When this happens, shift the approach. No matter how careful the planning, it is impossible to predict with certainty the reactions of different classes. An approach that has been successful with one group of learners will only trap an instructor into thinking it will be equally successful with another. No two teaching situations are identical.

The instructor may have three classes in the same subject, but each calls for its own unique lesson plan. The difference in the classes is represented in the three unique groups of learners. Only when the subject matter—not the learner—is the main concern can one lesson plan serve more than *one* class in a given subject. The ole pro is always alert to the differences in training situations.

Keep Lesson Plans Abreast of Recent Developments

Keep lesson plans up to date. After a lesson plan has been prepared, continuous revisions will be necessary since no two class populations are exactly alike. It may be necessary to make changes because:

1.   Learners vary
2.   Subject matter changes
3.   Training schedules change
4.   Instructional equipment is unavailable

5. New training equipment is available
6. Procedure changes

The instructor makes changes to meet the needs of his *immediate training situation.*

Lesson Plans Are Prepared for Use

A lesson plan will not work just because it looks well prepared in some standard form. To be a real aid in instruction, it must provide specific information in a convenient form. A usable lesson plan must supply data concerning the subject matter to be taught and the methods, procedures, and techniques of instruction to be followed in each step of the instructional process. Additional information that may be provided includes such items as time

limitations, lists of necessary supplies or tools, a listing of supplementary text references, and explanations of desired uses of equipment or machines. Other considerations are items such as method of presentation, training aids, and the training environment.

A good lesson plan turns bad when it is not used. The best of planning is to no avail if the instructor leaves the lesson plan at his desk while he is in class.

A good habit to develop is to review the lesson plan before class time. Few instructors are gifted with such memories that they do not need to refresh themselves on the materials and topics to be presented. A review will put what is to be taught uppermost in the mind, eliminate unnecessary pauses in the sequence of the presentation, and keep the lesson going as planned. After all, was not that the reason for all of the planning energy in the first place?

SUMMARY

REMEMBER, it is the planning that counts. Good lessons and classroom activities do not just happen—they must be planned. The best instructors begin by collecting answers to the important questions:*

1. What to teach?
2. How well am I acquainted with the subject matter chosen?
3. Who are the students?

*Denova, C.C. *The Executive's Guide to Training Employees in Business and Industry.* Chicago: The Dartnell Corporation, 1970.

4. What is their background?
5. What are the objectives of the course?
6. What do I want accomplished?
7. Am I going simply to present information or will I present problems in order to find solutions?
8. Will there be other speakers?
9. What are the major points I intend to make?
10. In what order?
11. How large a class do I expect?
12. How will I know that the objectives were met?

Systematic analysis provides the instructor with the structural framework for his course development. With this analysis, the instructor can select those tasks he will present and, therefore, he can identify all the materials he plans to use. When he has organized these materials and decides upon the teaching methods by which they will be presented, he will have the elements needed to develop the lesson plans for the course under development.

REMEMBER

A good presentation of a lesson does not just *happen;* it is very carefully *planned.*

6.
Teaching: That's What Instructors Do

Stating that teaching is what an instructor does is an oversimplification of his responsibility. Development of the trainees in skill, knowledge and attitude as needed by the business enterprise is the major responsibility of the individuals who conduct training. Teaching is helping individuals to learn. The instructor must act as a guide through what is the unknown or unfamiliar to the learner, because why should the learner stumble along the path when the easiest way is known by the instructor?

One of the differences between the "master-instructor" (or ole pro) and other teachers is that the "master" *is* a master of teaching skills and teaching knowledge that others do not have—or, if *the others* possess the skills and knowledge, they do not use them efficiently and effectively. Faced with a new difficult training situation, the "pro" can cope with the situation because he has the know-how and can apply it efficiently and effectively. Becoming a pro requires practice—practice based on theory. In fact, the professional development phase must be practiced in selecting and using the right theory.

This apprenticeship period requires three-quarters informa-

TELLING IS NOT TEACHING

tion mixed well with at least one-quarter (maybe more) intuition to equal one instructional decision. The skilled instructor is confronted with situations many times in a single class session, and it is his ability to increase his batting average that distinguishes him from the crowd of other instructors—*it makes him a professional.* These skills will permit the instructor to carry out his function—making decisions that will result in the most effective, efficient training possible.

Teaching is helping individuals to learn. It is not just the presenting of information. The instructor teaches *people* not subjects. In the final analysis, the test of how successful one's teaching has been is how well the student has learned. But before evaluation, comes educational method. Educational method is made up of tactics that will guide the learner most effectively through the course content. One cannot teach content without method, or vice versa. The basis of educational/training methodology is decision-making—*the selection of the strategy that will be best under the circumstances.* Thus, content is part of methodological strategy.

The decision-making process is influenced by still another variable—the learner. Each individual is unique. He has his own interests, abilities, attitudes, background, goals, potential *and* (as if these were not enough), he has his own style of learning. Consequently, if the instructional techniques used are to be successful with him, *they must be selected for him.*

Although methodological decision-making for particular education/training situations is contingent on many variables, a general pattern does seem desirable in most situations. The pattern usually found is:

1.   Diagnosis/Analysis
2.   Preparation
3.   Guiding the learner
4.   Evaluation of results
5.   Follow-up

Diagnosis
Diagnosis is the step in which the instructor determines what is to be done. Without good diagnosis, an instructor does not have an adequate basis on which to make a selection of teaching method or strategy. Diagnosis depends upon an analysis of all the known variables in the particular learning situation under consideration.

A major variable that affects instructional decisions is the objectives. There are two types of objectives:

1.   There are the overall objectives that influence the training programs in general. These are based on company objectives and do influence the type of curriculum and overall training or instructional strategy.

2.   There are the more specific objectives that influence the choice of content and instructional method per course and/or class session.

Another variable that determines instructional method is the nature of the subject matter—the course content. This includes not only the nature of the material but also its organization, and the company's (or training department's) philosophical base for teaching it.

Still another variable is the technology available. Technology includes training facilities, instructional techniques and the tools of teaching. The instructor who has a large repertoire of instructional techniques, backed up with a good store of instructional materials, equipment and facilities, has a distinct advantage over the instructor who has none of these assets. While it is becoming increasingly easy to acquire training paraphernalia, the trick is to select the right combination of techniques, materials and equipment for the specific occasion. The master-instructor does this effectively and efficiently.

One of the most important variables is the instructor himself. Like the learner, every instructor is an individual. He has strengths and weaknesses, likes and dislikes. Decisions invariably are influenced by one's background, inclination, ideals, attitudes, personality and competence. These individual differences in instructors cause individual differences in teaching style. An instructor will follow the style of teaching that he finds compatible. *It is right that he does*—within reason, of course.

Preparation

Since preparation can mean anything from opening the classroom windows to telling motivational jokes, it needs to be brought into focus. Preparation refers to the instructor getting himself ready to teach. Preparation includes the planning and organizing of instruction. An instructor should begin by answering these important questions:

1. What to teach?
2. How well am I acquainted with the subject matter chosen?
3. Who are the learners?
4. What is their background?

It's The
Planning
That Counts

5.   What are the objectives?
6.   Will there be other speakers?
7.   What are the major points I wish to make?
8.   In what sequence?
9.   How large is the class?
10. What training materials are available?
11. How will I know that the objectives were met?

The organization of instruction must begin with a well-thought-out plan. After a while, the diagnosis and the preparation steps tend to run together. The ole pro always performs them even though they are somewhat truncated.

The preparation phase includes preparing the trainee to receive the information. *Motivation* covers the essential active ingredient of this phase. Good preparation will create a readiness, eagerness or desire to learn on the part of the trainee. Creating *interest* is the best synonym for the motivational phase.

The idea of interest is one of the greatest doctrines regarding learning. Without the desire or the interest to learn, there will be little or no learning attained. Once interest is aroused, learning has

DON'T
BORE

a power supply. It can proceed under *learner power* instead of *instructor pressure*. Most important is the fact that if interest is kindled, learning will continue without demands from management.

The motivation phase includes the displaying of rewards in a manner so that they become meaningful and convincing to the worker. These may include such reasons as promotion, admiration from peers, escape from pain, preservation of life and other pay-offs for the individual. Each must see this for himself.

Good teaching does not consist of doing something to a person, but rather in motivating that individual to *do something.*

GOOD TEACHING
MOTIVATES TO DO!

No, That's Wrong; Use A 'Chute Next Time!

Guiding the Learner

Guiding learning includes the classroom activities—the presentation, the discussion, or whatever. Presentation covers whatever the instructor wishes to present to the trainee, but *good training* demands the presentation of what will bring forth the *desired* skill or ability to do the job. The end result is effective action of how to do something. The presentation phase, therefore, is essentially the phase in which the instructor gives direction. The word *direction* can be used in place of the less definite word—presentation.

The good instructor will select the appropriate path to meet a given training situation. The selection of the most effective path grows out of the total training situation—the objectives, the trainees, the subject matter, the training aids and materials available, and the instructor himself.

A wide variety of learner activities may be carried on in every type of training program. Frequently the measure of student learning is the extent of participation in activities related to the subject matter of the training program. Since the instructor has been "through" the subject matter before, he must act as a guide for the learner, pointing out the easy way through the "knowledge jungle" as well as indicating where the pitfalls are. Because a trainee must have experiences that give him a chance to practice the kind of behavior implied by an objective, the instructor must find a wide range of learning experiences.

Unless the instructions are clearly understood and correctly performed, instructor directions are useless. The directions must

be clearly grasped, and the reason or objectives free from doubt, if learner performance is to be good. Whatever is over the head of the trainee is wasted—wasted time, wasted effort and wasted money. Directions must be in simple language, or else the understandings of the trainee must be built up to the unknown by comparing it to enough of the known so that it is no longer a mystery.

EXPLAIN YOUR LANGUAGE

Words and analogies used by the instructor should have maximum meaning. Therefore, he must translate his presentation or directions into image-bearing words. Making meanings clear is the process of explaining. If instructors would explain more, trainees would get real meanings instead of a jumble of words and notes. They would be better prepared for the application phase, which is the real reason they are in training in the first place.

GOOD ADVICE
IS GOOD INSTRUCTION

The presentation phase not only gives clear directions, understanding and explanations, but also it gives advice. The doctor who merely describes the ailment to the patient is not giving advice. But if he tells the patient what to do, and what to take for his ailment, then the doctor is giving advice.

Demonstration or showing also may be part of the presentation phase. It is often the best and sometimes the only way to give meaningful directions. The use of pictures can aid in removing any language barrier that may exist between the instructor and the trainee.

Since the trainee is learning *how to do* things, the doing of those things by the instructor, before the eyes of the trainee as a sample to be initiated, ranks high in the developmental approach.

Demonstrations must be a model of performance, rather than to show off the instructor's ability.

Carefully planned demonstrations and carefully designed visualizations must help make directions clear. If they do not, there will be more waste.

WORTH HOW MANY WORDS?

The presentation should be continued until the ideas "click"—for the trainee, that is. Sometimes ideas come by degrees or by tedious fumbling. But, if the instructor is patient, it comes—remember, *it must come.* Unless it clicks, it is not *learned.* The trainee should not only feel that he has caught on, but the instructor should "see" that he does. The training loop is not complete until the ideas click for the trainee. The instructor has not really taught unless they do.

There is more to presenting information to a class than just presenting the information. The instructor must be sensitive to clues that the trainees will give while his class is in session. The instructor may have the technical information they need but if he does not understand the differences in individuals, the instructor will have considerable difficulty in getting the information across to the learners. Actually, to understand the trainees fully, the instructor must have a complete record of each of them. This is not practical since it is the general case that he will have them for only a short time. Consequently, the instructor must keep his eyes and ears wide open to learn as much as he can from his trainees. The better instructors concentrate particularly on those who fall in the extremes—fast learners and slow learners. They find out what makes a trainee slow, and give him individual attention. At the same time, the ole pro keeps the fast worker busy—provides him with more difficult types of assignments. While the instructor is concentrating on the fast and slow learners, he must not forget those who are in between—*all must be taught.* It may be difficult, but the instructor must try not to indicate favoritism. Because of the increased recognition of the importance of individual differences, the modern instructor should attempt to gear his teaching to the needs and abilities of the individual trainee in a variety of ways. Also, individual differences in learners must be cultivated, not corrected or tolerated. A wide variation exists in individuals and are equally prevalent regardless of the instructional method employed. Literally, the more an instructor teaches to his class, the more unlike they will become. This is due primarily to the fact that the limits of achievement for different persons vary greatly.

WATCH FOR CLUES

MEASUREMENT IS IMPORTANT

The Application of Learning

During the preparation phase, the instructor seeks to set the stage to increase the probability of learning. He seeks to get the trainee to want to do something. The presentation phase shows the trainee how to do that "something." The application phase gives the trainee the chance to do it in a trial situation. During this phase the trainee is put more or less on his own, because at some point the trainee must take over and try his ability *on his own.* The ability of the trainee to take over and proceed alone is the desired end result of all training.

Evaluation of Results

As an aid in differentiating between trainees, the instructor must use evaluating devices. Oral and written evaluations are valuable particularly when used in conjunction with observations of the individual. The instructor should watch for the trainees' reaction to each given lesson. An observant instructor can determine if his lesson is getting across to his trainees. When he sees doubt and confusion in the trainees, it is time for the instructor to consider if he has been going too fast, and if so, to slow down. Is the teaching method he has been using satisfactory or should he try to adjust it or try a new approach? A method of teaching may work wonders with one group of trainees and fall

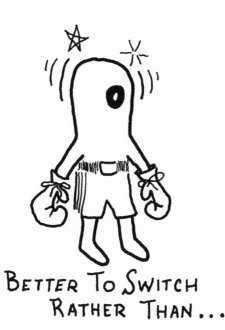

BETTER TO SWITCH
RATHER THAN...

short of the mark with another. Through experience and experimentation, the instructor will learn what teaching methods or techniques to use and when.

Not only should the performance of the trainees be evaluated, but the instructor must check to determine if he and the trainees have reached the objectives. If not, has he failed? It is failure only if the instructor refuses to recognize it as such. There can be no failures if the instructor evaluates early enough and applies remedial measures.

Frequent checks must be made for understanding. Asking the trainees, "Are there any questions?" will often bring no response. The instructor must take care not to interpret no response to this question to mean understanding. If there is no response, the instructor must ask one or two questions of his own. Newton's first law applies here: A body at rest tends to remain at rest, unless acted upon by some outside force. The instructor must provide the force necessary to place the body (trainee) into motion.

In the evaluation process, the instructor attempts to assess the success of his training sessions. Yet this is not a complete evaluation picture. To determine if the best, most economical training program was conducted, a diagnostic study of every aspect of training is a must. An effective evaluation plan must cover these three aspects:

1. *An assessment of the change in learner behavior.* Every avenue of trainee performance must be examined. There must be an analysis of his progress, and correlation between training evaluation and supervisory appraisal must be investigated.

2. *An analysis as to whether or not the training program furthers the achievement of organizational goals.* In business and industry, there is no other valid criterion for conducting training except an economic one. Every training effort, single course or entire program, must be analyzed for its potential profit contribution. If the training program does not result in a profit contribution, the investment in training cannot be economically justified.

3. *An evaluation of the training staff, methods and techniques.* The organization responsible for training must establish a reputation for employing and maintaining a highly qualified instructional staff. Therefore, evaluation of instructors, methods, techniques, materials, and programs must go on continuously.

Evaluation should be designed into the total program and should start at the time the training program is being planned. The development of the training program is not complete until standards of achievement are being attained. The standards vary according to the subject of the program. Tests to measure the degree of skill or competence achieved may be obtained or devised. Evaluating devices must be developed that measure the situation related to the particular field of the training program. An analysis plan for the evaluation of training programs in business and industry is not a simple process, nor is it an easy task if the job is to be done completely; but, the evaluation job must be done.

THE ROLE AND JOB OF THE INSTRUCTOR

Teaching is very much like selling. The instructor has his goods to sell, and there is no sale until the trainee buys. Therefore, the instructor must make the trainee want to buy. An instructor will have some trainees who think they do not want to learn. Some of these will consider the course material unimportant or impractical; others will merely lack interest.

Whatever the reason, individuals frequently come to the training sessions with no real desire to learn. Without this desire, they learn little. Therefore, an important part of an instructor's job is arousing in his trainees a genuine desire to learn. This involves showing a trainee that the personal rewards he can get from the material presented are worth the effort. In this sense, then, an instructor must be a salesman.

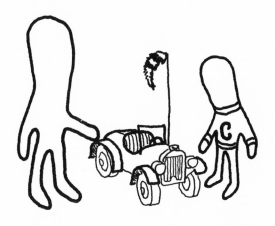

TRAINING IS SELLING

Pride

Probably more than any other single factor, an instructor's attitude toward teaching determines what kind of job he does and how much satisfaction and enjoyment he gets out of his work.

The instructor must, by example, show that he is proud of his job and the company he works for. He must not by word or action indicate that the training he is offering is anything but important. The instructor who approaches his class in an apologetic manner is certainly not offering the right kind of leadership.

Respect

The development of the attitude of respect is primarily a tactic of giving the trainee no chance to resent or criticize the instructor. The trainee will respect the instructor who "knows his stuff," shows ingenuity and initiative in putting it across, and is fair but firm in all of his relationships with his trainees. In short, the trainee expects the instructor to be aloof.

The instructor must take pride in keeping abreast of all new developments in his field and in being thoroughly informed about the workings of his company, especially that of his department.

Training in any situation provides an opportunity for many problems for the instructor. He may not have all the training materials that he would like to have, and the participants may not respond as planned. The instructor who can approach his job with enthusiasm (no griping regardless of the circumstances and especially to the trainees) and who uses his head and skill in devising ways and means of overcoming his situational problems

BECOME ATTACHED TO YOUR WORK

will develop in his trainees a respect for his ability and for that of his superiors.

DEVOUR INFORMATION

A point to remember is that it makes no difference how rigid the discipline, if it is consistent. Consistency makes for a happy situation. Consistency is more important than strictness or severity. If one knows at all times what can and cannot be done and what is and is not expected, he can adapt himself accordingly.

Once in a while a trainee will feel that he has been misjudged or discriminated against; or for some other reason he will have a grievance. The instructor must constantly be on guard against this sort of thing. As soon as the instructor becomes aware of these

Use Horse Sense

feelings, he should work with the trainee to help eliminate the grievance.

The instructor should accept personally the responsibility for the errors of the trainee, for, if the error is due to misunderstanding, the instructor is at fault for inferior instructions. *When wrong, admit it; when right, be humble.*

Trainees are in a training program to acquire the knowledge and skills required to perform an essential job for the company. They look to the instructor for guidance. If the instructor's guidance is to be of much help to a trainee, the instructor must be thoroughly familiar with the requirements of the position to which the trainee is assigned.

A LITTLE PRAISE HELPS

Be Friendly

People prefer to be called by their names, and trainees are no exception, so avoid any variation of the "hey you." If matching names with faces comes hard, the instructor should try one of these: make a list of names, use place cards or nametags, or prepare a seating chart.

When the trainees begin to arrive, they should be greeted with a smile. The instructor should introduce himself at the first meeting. Even though his name is on the chalkboard, it is necessary for the instructor to audibly mention his name so that the trainees will know how he wants it pronounced.

Enthusiasm

It is said that "enthusiasm is caught—not taught." The instructor who approaches his job with pride and vigor will find that his class will respond in a like manner. In addition, no one can be enthusiastic about anything that he feels is not important and useful. From an enthusiastic approach by the instructor, the trainees will develop:

(1)   desire to advance professionally,

(2)   pride in doing a job well, and

(3)   pride in doing more than is expected of them.

ENTHUSIASM Is CAUGHT...
NOT TAUGHT

AVOID MANNERISMS

Insincerity is easily detected by trainees and causes them to lose confidence in an instructor. Lack of instructor enthusiasm will cause even the best-planned training program to fall short of its objective.

Gestures

If the instructor is a chalk tosser, a floor walker, a window peeper, an ear puller and/or a whistler, he has something to learn about being a professional instructor. Any mannerism that does not emphasize the point being made is a distraction to the trainee.

Improper mannerisms are just as distracting to one trainee being trained on the job as they are to a group in the classroom.

Humor

The day is past when, like the Puritans, it was believed that training should be grim in order to be effective. However, there is still a big gap between humor and comedy. A joke, a play on words, or a pun is permissible when it is effective in directing attention or emphasizing a point. Any instructor who tries to be a comedian—who gets his class laughing *at* him rather than *with* him—is off-the-training-beam, to be sure.

WATCH YOUR LANGUAGE

Language

The instructor is not expected to conduct himself as if he were in a Sunday school class, but neither is he in the back room of Joe's bar. He will not prove himself to be a regular fellow by using curses and vulgar expressions. He may win a cheap type of popularity for the moment, but two things are more likely to happen: first, it will become increasingly harder for him to express himself clearly; and, second, his trainees will lose their respect for him as a man and a leader.

DON'T BLUFF

Bluffing Is Only for the Poker Table

A cardshark can "teach" the instructor a lesson at poker with a bluff. But the classroom is not a gambling room. There will be times when the instructor will not know all the answers. At such times, the proper procedure is to admit it. If the questions are important, however, the instructor must take some action toward finding out the answers. He must report back on his follow-up action. It is the immediate action to find the answers and the reporting back to the class that improves the instructor's integrity.

Usually it is a good practice to include the question in the lesson plan so that the instructor will have it the next time. Bluffing is dangerous for two reasons: first, the instructor probably won't get away with it; and second, the trainee may get the wrong or possibly dangerous information due to the bluff.

REMEMBER

When wrong, admit it;
When right, be humble.

Leadership

An instructor must be a good leader if he is to be deserving of his title. If an instructor is to be a good leader, his trainees must have confidence in him. The instructor cannot impart his feeling of confidence to his trainees unless he has confidence in himself. Many factors contribute to an instructor's self-confidence.

The first is to know thoroughly the subject or skill he is to teach. A confident instructor is not afraid to answer "I don't know" to a question; but if he does not know the answer, he must know where to find it.

The second factor that contributes to self-confidence is to have a clear-cut plan of action. It is here that a well thought out lesson plan proves its value.

A third contributing factor is to know the trainees, their backgrounds, their strengths, and their weaknesses. Instructional leadership also means the instructor must have control of the learning situation at all times. This means that the instructor has

CREATE AN IMPRESSION

the ability to guide the trainee's attention toward the proper points of learning as the lesson progresses and to prevent any distractions or wanderings from leading the trend of thought away from lesson objectives.

Before Learning Can Be Accomplished

Since all people do not respond to the same things, the instructor must study the participants and decide what would appeal to them. This appeal should be of such nature that it reaches everyone, approaches the objectives of learning, and builds worthwhile actions and purposes to reach the training goal.

FIRST, GET THEIR ATTENTION

Be Ready to Change

The instructor must be constantly aware of the reaction of the trainee and must make the adjustments as they become necessary. The instructor may find that a change-of-pace has a place in emphasizing or directing attention to a particular point. The pro is very sensitive to how he is coming across to his trainees. He constantly watches his class for signs which tell him that for some reason the class is in the dark; that there are no signs that the "click" has turned on the light of understanding.

The Physical Surroundings

The instructor must consider the physical environment in

which the teaching and learning processes will take place. Attention to the classroom is as important to the success of the lesson as the preparation of the lesson plan. The training environment can work for an instructor or it can work against him. The classroom can put the instructor and his trainees at ease or it can make everyone uncomfortable. The trainee lives in an environment during his training span. To him the atmosphere of

NEVER NEGLECT
PHYSICAL COMFORTS

the learning environment must be conducive to work and learning. Grambs and Iverson* describe the importance of this to learning:

> Just the way a classroom looks does much to build or weaken good management. Even if the classroom is not the most modern, if it is clean and neat, it will help set the tone of businesslike performance.

The instructor must check the physical conditions himself to determine that it is ready to receive the learners and that it and its furnishings are conducive to learning.

SUMMARY

Every instructor must remember that in the classroom he represents the company to the trainees. If the instructor has faults or shortcomings, the trainees will judge the company accordingly. Therefore, the instructor must always exercise good judgment.

If instruction is to be effective, the instructor must establish a receptive, cooperative relationship with the learners. The individuals must want to learn if they are to learn well. The burden is on the instructor to get his trainees into the proper mood to learn.

To accomplish this difficult assignment, the instructor must avoid the common errors:

1.   Not preparing a lesson plan.
2.   Not using the lesson plan prepared.

*Grambs, Jean D. and William J. Iverson. *Modern Methods in Secondary Education.* New York: The Dryden Press, 1952.

JUDGMENT

3. Poor lesson preparation.
4. Not getting the attention of the entire class.
5. Explaining only to the person making the mistake or asking the question, instead of the entire class.
6. Talking to those in front or to only one individual.
7. Talking in a low monotone.
8. Permitting to be side tracked.
9. Using words or phrases without explaining them.
10. Having distracting mannerisms.
11. Talking too rapidly or too slowly.
12. Carelessly writing or drawing on the blackboard.
13. Using sarcasm and profanity.
14. Neglecting the physical comforts of the class.
15. Talking down the nose at trainees.
16. Failing to admit, "I don't know," and not promising to find out.
17. Not maintaining equilibrium of temper.
18. Not using an accepted manner of addressing the trainees.
19. Failing to summarize frequently.
20. Failing to wear the proper attire.

7.

Establishing a Training Budget

What is a budget? A budget is a plan. It is a statement of expected results expressed in numerical terms. A training budget may be put in financial terms, man-hours, classroom-hours, student-hours, or instructor-hours; or it may reflect capital outlays and operating expenses. A good training forecast, therefore, becomes the basis for a good training budget.

A budget is an estimate of proposed expenditures for a given period and the proposed means of financing them. Linn* depicts the training budget as a triangle, with the educational plan forming the base, supporting the spending plan and financial plan sides. This emphasizes the important part that planning plays in estimating a budget. There must be a training plan to justify the expected expenditures for training. A training budget makes it possible to chart a future destination together with the means for arriving there.

*Linn, Henry H. *School Business Administration.* New York: Ronald Press, 1956.

WHO'S AFRAID OF THE BIG BAD BUDGET?

Since budgets are looked upon as control devices, many training administrators shake at the mere mention of *training budget*. All too often the subject of budgeting is avoided. Some training personnel shun budgets because of the belief (however mistaken) that they automatically lead to misery and a strait-jacketed financial existence.

Every training administrator must be budget oriented; so must his staff. This includes all members of the training department—yes, even the classroom instructor.

PLANNING
ELIMINATES
GUESSING

BUDGET: A SYNONYM FOR PLANNING

Making a budget is clearly a planning process, and it is the fundamental planning instrument in many companies for many training departments. A training budget forces a training administrator to make in advance a numerical expectation of cash flow, expenses (and possible revenues if involved in customer training), capital outlays and/or man-hour utilization. Since budgets are actually statements of plans, in financial or other terms, and are standards against which performance is measured, they are usually considered an instrument of control. A training budget is necessary for control, *but* it cannot serve as a standard for control unless it reflects the training plan. Although a budget usually implements a training program, it may actually be the program. A realistic forecast of an operating training plan reflects a sound and realistic budget.

If budgetary controls are to work, training managers (as well as top management of the enterprise in question) must remember that budgets are designed as tools and are not to replace the training management, that budgets have limitations and must be tailored to each different situation. No successful training budget can be truly "directed" by the management of a training department. To be most effective, the making and administration of a training budget must receive the support of top management.

Guesstimate: Another Synonym for Budget

A budget is an estimation of expenditures. It is the training administrator's best guess, and only that. It is not a concrete prediction of what must happen during the budgeted fiscal period. Past budgets and records of actual expenditures will prove helpful in preparing the current budget.

Limitations of a Training Budget

The preparation of a budget will not remove any training ills. The function of a budget is restricted, but it does provide an overview, an aid in analysis, and it helps in launching the training program into its future.

COLLECTING COST DATA

What is the worth of training? What does it cost not to train? Answering the first question with the second question is what most training administrators have been doing for years. It is time that serious consideration be given to the collection of valid cost data. Warren* suggests that the training cost data source should have four characteristics:

1. It must be readily available—ideally, from an existing system, such as payroll records, time cards, purchase orders, expense records, etc.

2. It must provide the data in a form consistent with other sources reporting similar data: if time-card data reported for manpower budgeting does not utilize fringe costs, it would be useless to include these costs in training actions.

3. It must provide complete data: all transactions must be included in the system. Thus if trainee time is to be an item, there must be some assurance that time will be reported on all participants. Or, in another situation, if purchases of software are

*Warren, Malcolm W. *Training for Results.* Reading, Massachusetts: Addison-Wesley Publishing Company, 1969.

included, they should account for all items, even those bought out of petty cash.

4.   It must be able to control the inputs it receives and maintain records from which meaningful reports can be made. Lack of backup records usually results in missing information. Without all necessary data, measures of training cost will continue to be estimates at best and creative writing at worst.

Collecting cost data must be along these lines:

1.   Cost of research, development and planning of programs.

2.   Cost of the administration and support of the programs. The major cost for support will be for the personnel who conduct the training—training staff or outside the training department (in-company or outside consultant).

3.   Cost of persons taking the training including wages or salaries during training, and travel and living expenses.

4.   Cost of space, materials, equipment, maintenance, utilities and other expenses. Collecting all this data is necessary to gain cost experience for cost estimating. Once experience provides a cost breakdown system which is useful to the training administrator, he will be able to estimate future actions along with their cost within tighter tolerances.

THE BULLET MUST BE BIT

It is not too much to expect of a training director to require him to itemize the cost of training activities. Some companies go a step further; they expect him to provide a cost estimate of future training activities. There are a few organizations that expect a forecast of return on the dollars invested in training.

Each training administrator must develop his budgeting system to conform to his company's requirements and philosophy. It is difficult to forecast and plan training programs, including cost estimates, if the training director does not have full control and responsibility of the expenditures of all training dollars.

BUDGET PREPARATION

Many things can influence the preparation of a training budget. As the training administrator analyzes his particular requirements, he must take into account these general considerations:

1.   What is the financial position of the organization? This is a major overall factor. The company's economic status will influence his ability to plan an extensive training program. He may be forced to plan training activities on a selective basis.

2.   Where is the company located? There are two additional considerations possible. First, is the company in a large or small community? If the business enterprise is in a small community, emphasis on its community relations and responsibility in the field of education and training may be great. Second, is the outside-the-plant educational and training opportunity large or small? If it is possible to use educational programs and facilities off-site, it may be more economical to do so.

3.   What is the company type, including its type of organization and the type of personnel? Is the organization mainly staff or mainly line? Is management dominant or passive? (MOST IMPORTANT: Are they sold or unsold on training activities?) Are

employees mainly professional or not, skilled or unskilled, male or female, old or young, tenured or relative newcomers? Are employees organized as union labor or not? Is the union aggressive or considerate?

4.   What are the products and/or services of the enterprise? The type of product and/or service has a definite effect on the type of training activities. Is the business one of production, merchandising, or servicing? Will boom times or depression or the seasons have an effect on the business?

    REMEMBER!

Budget forecasting is a synonym
for training planning.

The foregoing questions are not answerable according to any given principle of management. Much depends on the particular situation in which the training administrator finds himself. Other considerations partially implied in the above list are the attitude and progressiveness of top management, the established policies and procedures, the overall size of the company and the historical background. How the training director evaluates the relative importance of each is dependent on the situation at the time of budget preparation and *his personality*. The important consideration is that he must evaluate them *before* he considers the problem of proper budget forecasting.

SUMMARY

A budget can be friend or foe, an enemy to be dreaded yearly or a valuable co-worker for the training process. The training personnel have it within their power to use, misuse, or fail to use the budget as a functional tool. The need for a budget will not go away if ignored. But it will prove to be a valuable planning process as the training director moves to increase his department's service to the trainees and to management.

There is no quick and easy way to prepare a budget for training activities. This does not mean that estimates cannot be made; it means that the training director must weigh carefully each expenditure, and he must seek out accurate benchmarks that will aid him in estimating the cost of actions to take place in the future.

The company's accounting philosophy has a direct influence on the manner in which the training budget will be prepared. For example, if trainee time is to be accounted for, the dollar cost of trainee time spent during training activities must be charged somewhere. Not only must the training director know *where,* but the benefiting department must also know if their account will be charged for the development of "their" employees.

Since there are as many idiosyncrasies to budget-making as there are companies that operate with a budget, it would be impossible to present here a recipe for the ideal budget for the support of training activities. It is possible, however, to suggest what must be identifiable in order to maintain a total accounting of the actual cost of training.

It is an arduous task to establish a special accounting system only for the training department. But, if the training administrator can identify the data sources that will aid him in preparing a true picture of the cost of training, surely he is sophisticated enough to fit this data to the form required by his company.

8.

Evaluating Training Activities

An evaluation program of training in business or industry is not a simple process, nor is it an easy task if the job is to be done completely. The evaluation must determine what changes in the employee have taken place as the result of exposure to experiences called "training." An analysis must be made to determine if the best, most economical training program was conducted. A diagnostic study of training methods and techniques is in order to determine whether or not organizational effectiveness has been attained.

Evaluation of training, therefore, generally has three major aspects:

1.   An assessment of the change in employee behavior.

2.   An analysis as to whether or not the training program furthers the achievement of organizational goals.

3.   An evaluation of the training personnel, methods and techniques.

LEARNER EVALUATION

One of the important steps in the learning process is the periodic measurement of the progress of trainees and the evaluation of the results of a training program. Most training is evaluated by written test, performance test and/or observance of practical exercises being accomplished by the trainee. Tests have value to the trainees for the following reasons:

1.   Test scores show the trainee what progress he is making—they measure his achievement. He can compare his work with that of other trainees, as well as with his own previous work.

2.   Tests identify the parts of the course in which the trainee is weak—they diagnose his difficulties.

3.   Tests cause the trainee to review work, which helps him to organize and retain knowledge—they measure his understanding.

4.   Tests give the trainee practice in the application of fundamental principles to varying problem situations.

5.   Tests help the trainee to distinguish between the relevant and the irrelevant.

6.   Tests give the trainee a better conception of the objectives of the course—they may give insight to company objectives.

7.   Tests can stimulate the lagging trainee to make a greater effort—they give incentive.

Importance of Learner Evaluation

The value of training methods and materials during the instruction are unknown until their effects are measured. Measurement is essential to the trainee's progressive learning capacity. If a learner's abilities and capabilities are not measured, a knowledge of him is impossible.

A test is a measuring instrument. The designer of a measuring device must know what can be measured.

Achievement tests are frequently given for the purpose of "grading" trainees. They should be given even more frequently for the purpose of discovering gaps in learning so that any "must know" ideas or skills can be retaught and future instruction can be improved.

Tests can be very helpful in assisting the learner to improve his skill and understanding. Tests should always be prepared and administered with the idea in mind that they are effective teaching devices. In order to accomplish this purpose, the instructor must review each test thoroughly after the papers have been scored and returned to the trainees. It is important that this be done as soon as possible after the administration of the test in order that incorrect thinking by trainees may be corrected as early as possible.

Any *good* test is valid, reliable and mechanically simple. If tests are to be used for grading trainees, they must also be discriminating, comprehensive, as objective as possible, and cover a range of difficulty. The most important of these characteristics is validity.

PROGRAM EVALUATION

A manufacturing plant would soon be out of business if it did not check up on its product at various stages in the production process. Similarly, no training program can be operated efficiently without frequent and accurate checks. The individuals responsible for the training programs must conduct surveys to determine what is the impact on the company product(s) and/or company services as well as the participants in the various training programs.

Production output is of prime importance. The company production process should be checked for trainee contribution to useful production versus waste, and level of production of the trained employee versus the untrained; quality control should be checked. There should be an analysis of the employee's progress, and the correlation between training evaluation and supervisory appraisal should be investigated.

It's the Answers That Are Important

An ostentatious list of questions may be impressive to some, but they do not get the job done. A worthy decision must be based upon the answer, not the questions.

What is the worth of training? To answer this question, there must be articulation and communication between the instructors and supervisory personnel. Follow-ups must be conducted. These should consist of interviewing trainees as well as supervisors to help determine ways of changing and improving the training program as necessary. Supervisors must be consulted for their observations of trainee performance on the job. (After all, job performance is the prime objective of training programs in business and industry.) The comparison of test results by the supervisor and the instructor will assist greatly in keeping the supervisor-instructor discussion focused on the *trainee* needs and methods to meet them rather than on instructor and/or supervisory shortcomings.

"What does it cost not to train?" is the retort of training

directors. But they must compare "real" cost. They must compare the cost of training to the value of the expected results. At this point, whether to train or not becomes clear. For example, a training effort aimed at improving supervisory performance reviews may cut turnover and, therefore, recruiting costs. What are these man-hours and advertising cost worth? Comparing cost MUST be along these lines:

1. Cost of the person taking the training and cost of the person giving the training, including pay during training, travel and living expenses.

2. Cost of space, materials, maintenance, utilities and other expenses, including amortized cost of program preparation and equipment.

The idea here is that when cost data are collected, the data on the TOTAL cost must be collected. A decision made from such data can weather the storm of budget contraction that frequently scuttles many training activities.

The most important answer is to *this* question:

> *Will what the participants do after the training program result in a profit contribution or cost savings in excess of the cost of the training?*

If the answer is "no," the investment in training (single course or program) is not economically justified. In business and industry, are there other valid criteria for training besides an economic one? *No!* Every training effort must be analyzed for its potential return at some point in time. The earlier the return, the easier the justification.

Tests and the Instructor

A test can be used as a pre-instructional device. To make the instruction valuable, it is necessary to determine the level at which the trainee should begin the course. No matter what arguments are advanced to the contrary, the fact remains that the individuals chosen for a particular class are the ones to be trained. Whatever their shortcomings and limitations, it seems reasonable to start where *they* are. A few words of description will aid in determining where they are in regard to knowledge. This procedure is a *must* in training programs where the learners entering have varying amounts of skill and occupational experience. Pre-instructional testing is particularly useful in determining if the prerequisites have been met.

Workers seek to improve themselves by learning the advanced skills and techniques in their occupations. If they are required to begin their learning process at a level of work at which they believe they are already competent, they will be uninterested in the training program. Similarly, if they are assigned work that is beyond their ability, they will become discouraged and will lose interest.

The value of tests to the instructor is as follows:

1.   Tests show the instructor whether or not his presentation of the subject is sufficiently effective to accomplish the objective of the course.

2.   Tests enable the instructor to compare the effectiveness of different teaching methods.

3.   Tests show the instructor which points he did not make clear, thus enabling him to go back and clarify these points.

4.   Tests enable the instructor to give personal attention and guidance to the trainees who are experiencing difficulty with the subject.

5.   Tests can be used as a measure of achievement to determine whether or not the trainee has learned enough about

the subject to satisfy the certificate or promotional standards of the company.

There are some factors which may affect test results:

1. The physical and mental condition of the learner when he takes the test.
2. The physical and mental condition of the instructor when he constructs the test and when he scores it.
3. The difference in the psychological effects on the learner when taking a test.
4. The element of chance which helps some and hurts others.
5. The difference in scoring by different instructors.

Measure of Learning Difficulties

Tests can be used to discover the particular elements of the lesson content in which the trainee is weak and needs additional help. By means of tests, the instructor can discover why learning has not resulted from the training activity of the learner. The instructor must enable the trainee to understand why his learning is incomplete, as determined by the test, if the difficulty is to be overcome. In other words, if lesson content was important enough to be measured by a test, and if the trainee failed to demonstrate mastery, then *that* element of the lesson must be made clear to the learner.

PERSONNEL, METHODS AND TECHNIQUES EVALUATION

If management accepts training as one of the necessary tools for an efficient operation of the company, evaluation of the training programs conducted must be given serious attention. The training programs must be evaluated to determine:

1.   If objectives are being attained.

2.   How well the results of training programs are filling the organizational needs.

3.   Are the dollars being spent on training producing the results needed?

4.   What improvements can be made in training?

5.   Was training "really" necessary in this area or situation?

The evaluation of training programs is not a simple task, since we are dealing with the measurement of human behavior, or the measurement of the results of human behavior. We are trying to determine what changes, if any, have taken place in skills, knowledge and attitudes of employees as a result of an experience called "training." When management views training as a *management tool* and asks how well this *tool* is being used, research ingenuity must be utilized to answer the inquiry.

The organization responsible for training programs must establish a reputation for employing and maintaining a highly qualified instructional staff. Basic to the retention of such a staff is a personnel evaluation program which begins with the initial selection and continues throughout the professional life of the instructor. Essentially, instructor evaluation is one of the strongest forces for the improvement of instructional methods and techniques. It is premised on the fact that instructors must move forward in their professional contribution and in service to employees. The evaluation process is an orderly method under which staff members may consciously improve their service to the company.

The tests can be used to inform the instructor as to how successful he has been in accomplishing the objectives of the lesson, course, or program. Every test is a measure of the instructor's skill. Training activity and instruction can be improved only if the points at which they have failed are clearly recognized by the instructor. If a test shows that a number of the trainees are weak in one or more elements of the lesson, it is clear that the instructor must examine:

1. The methods used to present the elements,
2. The training activity used to provide practice in their use, and
3. The learner's readiness for the elements presented.

Evaluation of instructors, methods, techniques, classes and programs is done by almost everyone; it goes on continuously. Evaluation should be designed into the total training program. It should start at the time the program is being *planned*. Evaluation has value throughout the training program. Evaluation of results is a process of assessing the adequacy and suitability of proficiencies developed through training as defined by performance requirements of the job and as measured by performance on the job.

Valid and specific behavioral objectives are necessary if training is to be properly evaluated. There must be a standard by which to measure. Evaluation of training results must be based on a comparison of performance before the training with performance after training.

Is Evaluation Necessary?

The planning process for training programs is not complete without a specific plan for training evaluation. An evaluation plan is necessary in order to be able to report on the effectiveness of the training program. A follow-up of the learners is necessary to determine how effectively they are using their training on the job.

The training evaluation serves as a means of improving instruction, uncovers the need for remedial training, and may open avenues to new training in an entirely different area of need.

Who should conduct the evaluation follow-up? Denova* found that an unexpected phenomenon occurred when the training evaluation follow-up was conducted by the participants' supervision rather than the training department's personnel. He found that this procedure would ensure that supervision would make additional observations and have several personal contacts with its subordinates. These additional observations strengthen the employee performance evaluation and tend to influence the general motivation factors for employees, which in turn would have a bearing on their productivity and behavior. In short, Denova found that the Hawthorne Effect was produced when the training evaluation follow-up was conducted by management.

A Word of Caution Regarding Evaluations

Training is a vitally serious matter for any company. Personnel responsible for training programs should never lose sight of the fact that the primary objective of training is to make better employees. All too often, training personnel in a search for the best way to train will stress in their evaluation techniques the question of whether the trainees liked the course or program. The emphasis then is shifted from the question of whether the training program produced better employees to the question of whether the participants *enjoyed the course.*

*Denova, Charles C. "Training Evaluation Causes Change in Behavior." *Personnel Administration.* September-October, 1969, pp. 55-56.

A practical, hard-headed top management must concentrate on those methods of evaluation which show how much better the employees are doing *as a result of the training received.*

IS THERE ANY OTHER WAY
TO RUN A TRAINING GROUP?
You bet there's not!

SUMMARY

To determine if the best, most economical training program was conducted, a diagnostic study of every aspect of the training is a must. An effective evaluation plan generally has three major aspects:

1. *An assessment of the change in employee behavior.* Every avenue of employee performance must be examined. There should be an analysis of the employee's progress, and the correlation between training evaluation and supervisory appraisal should be investigated. After the training program, the profit contribution or cost savings must be compared as the results of the change in behavior of the participants.

2.   *An analysis as to whether or not the training program furthers the achievement of organizational goals.* In business and industry, there is *no* other valid criterion for conducting training (single courses or program) besides an economic one. Every training effort *must* be analyzed for its potential profit contribution. If the training does not result in profit contribution or cost savings, the investment in training is not economically justified.

3.   *An evaluation of the training personnel, methods, and techniques.* The organization responsible for training must establish a reputation for employing and maintaining a highly qualified instructional staff. Evaluation of instructors, methods, techniques and programs must go on continuously. Evaluation should be designed into the total program and should start at the time the program is being planned.

An analysis plan for the evaluation of training programs in business or industry is not a simple process, nor is it an easy task if the job is to be done completely. But, the evaluation job *must* be done.

The preceding paragraphs in this Summary are stated also in the first chapter of this book, in order to emphasize the importance of effective evaluation in any training effort.

9.
Research: The Untapped Frontier

The importance of research in the field of industrial training must be recognized more widely, and steps must be taken to develop research commensurate with the training needs. In this era of rapid technological change, many things are occurring that affect occupational education and development of the labor force. New concepts are emerging. New materials, processes and machines are appearing—some replacing older ones. Significant changes are taking place in the characteristics and spread of the population. These changes, and many others, have an effect on job education and training.

MEETING THE NEED

If occupational education and training is to meet the needs of this rapidly changing society, it must adapt itself to the changing conditions. The training patterns of organizations must fit themselves into the evolving structure of the environment. Curriculum must be in line with the technological changes and the social needs. The methods of instruction must be in keeping with the latest and best understanding of how people learn and how they can be taught more effectively.

Research has been conspicuous by its absence in the field of training. Little investigation has been made of the labor market and the types of training programs required to satisfy those needs. Research of an evaluative type, which is fundamental to sound program development, has been very limited. Little or no evidence has been gathered regarding the results or effectiveness of the instruction given, and various rationalizations and excuses have been offered for the inadequate statistics.

If training programs are to provide adequately for the needs of business and industry as a whole, or if specific programs are to be effective, much more information is needed than is now available. This is the task of research.

To conduct training programs without an analysis of needs, direction and means is unthinkable. The training administrator carries out this analysis as the normal routine of his duties and responsibilities.

In the past there has been a lack of enthusiasm on the part of training staffs to acquire the basic skills and tools for systematic problem solving. As McGehee points out:

> The failure to make adequate evaluation of training techniques and methods arises from two sources. First, training personnel by and large are not acquainted with the exact methods of controlled research and statistical techniques. Second, and perhaps even more important, industrial executives have not been indoctrinated into the necessity of careful evaluation of training as well as personnel activities.[1]

The Need for Research to be Industrially Oriented

There is a definite need for training research to be oriented towards business and industry. Difficulties arise whenever we try to apply the results of laboratory research to the industrial setting:

FIRST, the subjects used are generally rats, monkeys, or pigeons and when humans are involved, they are most often students in a school environment—secondary school or college. For the learning theorist and behavioral psychologist, such subjects and environments are quite appropriate. But the motives, the reactions, the incentives and the abilities involved in an industrial training environment differ in a number of unspecified ways.

SECOND, the criterion of learning employed is most often quite arbitrary, and is generally below that required in the industrial setting. Very few laboratory experiments have required the subjects to perform the learned task over many months or years. If they did, would the principles studied need to be modified?

THIRD, in a laboratory situation, the tasks to be learned are quite simple, and are generally below those required in industry. Contrast the learning of a list of nonsense syllables or the running of a maze with the learning of the procedures and skills required to become an electronic component solderer or the operator of a lathe.

FOURTH, much of what is currently happening in company training programs is based on studies of original learning. The maintenance of behavior on the job involves different principles. To this extent, the transferring of training most efficiently to the job situation may also require different or modified principles. Until systematic research is done in business and industrial environments, using business and industrial motives, incentives and rewards, we will continue to operate in the dark.

Scope of Training Research to Date

The scope of research projects carried out in industrial training has been narrow. All too often, in business and industrial training programs, only one type of research (if it can be called research) has been stressed—*program planning.* Even here, there has been a tendency to conduct such surveys only once—when the training program is begun. It is regrettable that this activity, such as it is, is not repeated periodically.

Operations research and evaluation in training and education have been too often nonexistent except in theses for college degrees. Unfortunately, this research has been, in the main, confined to vocational education as it applies to public school systems, and is largely unrelated to the business and industrial community. In addition, it covers too little ground to add much to new knowledge. Some general observations concerning this research indicate that:

a.   Much of the activity has been applied research.

b.   There has been little research conducted under controlled conditions.

c.   For the most part, the research has been superficial, with little depth or penetration.

d.   Little attention has been paid to disciplines such as the psychology of learning in the business environment or human relations in the occupational setting.

e.   Information concerning experimentation (trying new ideas) has had limited circulation.

The reasons why research in industrial training has followed such a pattern may be outlined as follows:

1.   Most training directors are pragmatists, interested mainly in the tasks they are held responsible for, rather than in research.

2.   Few individuals have been trained for research in industrial training and education.

3.   Much of the research has grown out of the requirements for graduate degrees in vocational education; therefore, most of it is non-business oriented.

4.   Comprehensive research requires facilities and financing, which top management has been unwilling to provide.

The Scope Needed for Tomorrow

A comprehensive research program would entail both large and small studies. It would cover all the fields of occupational education, and deal with aspects within the various types of training programs within these fields. Many studies would deal with applied research growing out of current problems. Such a comprehensive program could include activity that would bring together findings from disciplines such as psychology, sociology and economics in an attempt to define a technology of training or a system for training and education.

The main purpose of research in training is obvious—*the improvement of the efficiency of the training.* The course of action is to examine critically *every* facet of the training system:

need for training
objectives of training
programs conducted
participants in training
training instructors
training management
company efficiency through training

employee efficiency through training
and many others.

The objective of any training program, according to De-Phillips, Berliner, and Cribbin,[5] "is to change human behavior in a predetermined direction aimed at the improvement of the efficiency of the company." This change will be reflected in employee attitude, knowledge, and skill.

Research also aids in the development of a training system by furnishing critical and analytical evidence that make sound managerial decisions possible. In other words, a rigorous, logical process of collecting training data will reduce the probability of failure to make sound training decisions in areas that include:

1. Is training necessary?
2. What training is required?
3. Where is it required?
4. To whom should it be presented?
5. When and how long should the program be—including length and number of each session?
6. How should it be done?
7. By whom should it be conducted?
8. Was the training efficient?
9. How well were the training personnel prepared?

With regard to the problem of evaluating the efficiency of training to determine the best, most economical program, De-nova[2] suggests that an effective evaluating plan has three major aspects:

1. *An assessment of the change in employee behavior.* Every avenue of employee performance must be examined. There should be an analysis of the employee's progress, and the correlation between training evaluation and supervisory appraisal

should be investigated. After the training program, the profit contribution or cost savings must be compared as the results of the change of the participants.

2. *An analysis as to whether or not the training program furthers the achievement of organizational goals.* In business and industry there is *no* other valid criteria for conducting training (single courses or program) except an economic one. Every training effort *must* be analyzed for its potential profit contribution. If the training does not result in a profit contribution or cost savings, the investment in training is not economically justified.

3. *An evaluation of the training personnel, methods and techniques.* The organization responsible for training must establish a reputation for employing and maintaining a highly qualified instructional staff. Evaluation of instructors, methods, techniques, and programs must go on continuously. Evaluation should be designed into the total program and should start at the time the program is being planned.

AREAS OF CONCENTRATION
RECOMMENDED FOR RESEARCH

A crucial area of research is that of the application of learning principles and theories to practice. Industrial trainers tend to embrace academic principles *without question.* There is the tendency during program planning to think in terms of *time* increments instead of learning increments, i.e., how short can the course be before overlearning takes place, and how do we find out the trainee has overlearned? Every trainee has to be motivated to learn. If we use a schedule reinforcement in training, how will this affect his reaction to that which he will receive from his supervisor on the job?

The scope of training research can be a long list of specific questions for which specific research might provide answers. The following few questions are representative of studies needed:

1.   What modifications of teaching methods are desirable in training the unemployed worker, the youth with special problems and other special groups?

2.   How effective are the various types of specific instructional aids in supervisory and technical training programs?

3.   What criteria are most useful in the selection of trainees for specific training programs?

4.   What programs should be conducted in business and industry as compared with what vocational schools should teach?

The field of the relevancy of education and training to job motivators is fair game for training research in business and industry.

Change in behavior would be expected to appear whenever anyone participates in a learning experience. These changes *seem* to be peculiar to the population participating, to the material to which the participants are exposed, to the training method used and to the personality of the instructor conducting the program. There is a question as to the degree of behavior change that would occur if variables such as skill training, supervisor counseling, instructor follow-up, and wages were isolated.[3] The amount or direction of behavioral change may be limited by these peculiarities—and others; *we don't really know for sure.*

Management should give more attention to training the worker in areas other than those of a technical nature. Further research is needed deemphasizing skill development as the *primary* determiner of the worker's performance. Employee attitudinal aspects may outweigh skill development and mastery. Research is needed to determine which employee attitudes are controllable and which have the greatest impact on production. This would tie in with the notion that labor and management have not tapped the full potential of employee resources. Research concentrated in this area could determine not only how to tap the employee resource potential but how to do so efficiently and profitably for business and industry.

WHO SHOULD CONDUCT TRAINING RESEARCH?

Everyone who is responsible for a training function is concerned with the operating effectiveness of his program; but research techniques for determining such effectiveness have been almost entirely unused. The reason given most often is that there is a lack of qualified personnel in training departments to conduct the research required.

The idea of conducting training research seems to produce the same reaction in training personnel as does formulating a training budget—fear. What is needed is a change in the state of mind of administrative personnel—primarily, the training director. Kettering has pointed out what is a more practical approach:

> Research is a high-hat word that scares a lot of people. It needn't. It is rather simple. Essentially, it is nothing but a state of mind—a friendly, welcoming attitude toward change. Going out to look for change instead of waiting for it to come. . . It is the composer mind instead of the fiddler mind; it is the 'tomorrow' mind instead of the 'yesterday' mind.[4]

Research can be conducted effectively by the instructors in industrial and business environments. Unheard of? Maybe so! But, who is often responsible to update and improve the curriculum? The instructor. But, curriculum revision must be guided by evidence found in significant and relevant data, is the reply. OK, but who is asked to collect this data? Right again: The instructor.

Research is the *technique* by which these data can be collected, organized and analyzed. From this procedure comes a more intelligent decision as to what and how to improve or update existing curriculum.

GETTING THE INSTRUCTOR INVOLVED IN RESEARCH

The instructor who is teaching a full schedule, and in addition has various non-instructional duties, may indicate that he is not interested in research. He may insist that he is too busy with other things. Most instructors can find *some* justification for not engaging in research.

That is where supervisors and members of management can play an important role. If we are asking the instructors to be responsible for the best program possible, why not ask that the data necessary to evaluate their curriculum be collected and analyzed in an orderly fashion? (Is this any way to define Research? *You bet it is!*)

Once instructors become involved, many of them will gain much satisfaction from participating in research. They will focus their attention on the problems and issues. This exercise will establish various alternatives from which a solution is selected. In addition, and most important, the instructors will become more cognizant of problem areas in their specialized fields.

KEEPING ABREAST THROUGH RESEARCH

The instructor has the responsibility of keeping abreast of the technological changes in the field covered by his curriculum. Therefore, individual courses and training programs must be constantly evaluated, revised and refined.

Even though he may not render the final decision on specific courses to be added or deleted from the curriculum, the instructor has the opportunity to obtain the facts that warrant change. An obvious way to decide upon alternatives is to try them and see what happens. Such experimentation is used in scientific inquiry, especially in view of the intangible factors. The most generally used and certainly a most effective technique in curriculum decision making is research and analysis. Although the lessons of experience may be drawn upon in analyzing and although experimentation may be undertaken to test hypotheses, research and analysis have many advantages for weighing courses of action.

In the first place, the solution of the problem requires that it be broken into its component parts, and the various tangible and intangible factors studied. In the second place, study and analysis are likely to be far cheaper than experimentation.

AMOUNT OF RESEARCH EFFORT

The principle of limiting factor may apply to the amount of effort expended. This is nowhere more applicable than in the case of business and industrial training research. Not every business or industrial training program can stand the cost or delay of careful analysis and weighing of alternative hypotheses. Therefore, the most avid researcher must tailor his explorations to fit the available time.

OBSTACLES TO RESEARCH IN TRAINING

The obstacles that interfere with the conduct of research in business and industrial training programs vary from financial limitations to the personality traits of the personnel conducting the research. The largest obstacle in the path of research in training is top management's interpretation of profit and efficiency. Therefore, very little money has been available to support research in training. Many members of top management view training research as a waste of company funds. Companies spend millions of dollars each year on research that is concerned with technological advances, but spend "pennies" on research with regard to human behavior.[5]

Top management (including the training director) has not been committed to the necessity of training research in business and industry. But training research requires cooperation of every level of the management team—top management to the lowest level of operating supervisor. Cooperation when participation is required has been slow in coming. Many levels of supervision often feel that it is an imposition on their time and an interference with their work schedule.

In this regard, the personnel responsible for training programs (and therefore training research) have been at fault also. Training directors have failed to be practical and have not been considerate of the operating manager's work schedule and load. Such actions tend to clash with staff and operational managers and the training director, therefore, is sometimes viewed as "too academic and too theoretical."

Most of the research thus far has been superficial, with little depth or penetration, and relatively little research has pulled together different disciplines that have bearing on business and industrial training, e.g., economics, psychology, sociology, and labor market analysis.

To offset the obstacles confronting training research, DePhillips, Berliner, and Cribbin[5] recommend the following:

1. Change the attitudes of management toward research.
2. Give research in training the high status it requires.
3. Provide the financial backing it deserves.
4. Generate the cooperation and coordination of all levels of the management team.
5. Educate for an appreciation of the importance of research.
6. Train the training directors in the tools and methods of research, as well as train researchers to understand the limitations and problems of management.

REPORTING RESEARCH AND DEVELOPMENT

A study of business and industrial training is severely handicapped by inadequate reporting and a lack of sufficient evidence to make an adequate evaluation of its methods or achievements. Information is generally not available concerning the number of trainees who complete programs, and even less statistical information is available regarding their success after completion of training. Therefore, conducting research is not enough. Collecting data, evaluating it, and selecting from alternative courses of action for your internal training program is not enough. This knowledge and experience *must be shared.* The best way is to publish experience. Yes, there will be those individuals who will criticize aspects of *your* research, but you must have the fortitude to say, "If you can do better, go right ahead." And if they can, *they should.* In this way, we will have a continuing refinement of the training system in business and industry.

Research and program development must be encouraged. The results of training research and development must be made available on a nationwide basis.

TRAINING RESEARCH AND THE FUTURE

One of the most challenging areas of the future is that of obtaining more real research and development in business and industrial training and techniques. The level of research effort and support is low. There are several reasons for this. General research in business and industrial training is a difficult field, exceedingly complex and dynamic. It is one where facts and relationships are hard to come by and where the controlled experiment of the laboratory is difficult.

In undertaking this type of research, patience and understanding are needed. Perfection of analysis to include all kinds of variables is a laudable goal for the researcher. Occupation and skill training programs are surely sufficiently well established and accepted to allow a questioning and discriminating attitude about their practices, procedures, techniques and even the *programs* themselves. But research without development is insufficient. One of the major challenges for the training researcher of the future is the need for developing more training innovations. This would place more alternatives in the hopper to be tested in order that the *best* be chosen.

Although a considerable amount of research has been carried out, it falls short of meeting current needs of business and industry. Research projects in occupational education have largely been confined to the normative-survey type, with little attention paid to experimental research under controlled conditions. Some compilations of completed projects have been made—largely graduate student theses in vocational education—but no comprehensive reporting has been done, especially in the trade journals of business and industry.

REFERENCES

1. McGehee, William. "Persistent Problems in Training." *Current Trends in Industrial Psychology.* Pittsburgh: University of Pittsburgh Press, 1949.

2. Denova, Charles C. "Is This Any Way to Evaluate a Training Activity? You Bet It Is!" *Personnel Journal,* July 1968, p. 493.

3. Denova, Charles C. *An Assessment of the Effect on Self-Confidence of the Acquisition of New Skills.* Unpublished dissertation for Doctorate, from U.C.L.A., 1968.

4. Kettering, C.F. "More Music Please, Composer." *Saturday Evening Post,* Vol. CCXI (1938), p. 32.

5. DePhillips, F.A., W.M. Berliner & J.J. Cribbin. *Management of Training Programs.* Homewood, Illinois: Richard D. Irwin, Inc., 1960.

10.

Must Customer Training
Be Autonomous?

This chapter is for those companies that are planning to have or that currently have more than one autonomous function responsible for training—generally one for employee development and another for customer development.

The section of the enterprise responsible for the development and/or familiarization of buyers with the company products or services is generally referred to as Customer Services or Customer Training. The grouping of activities to reflect a paramount interest in the customer is commonly found in a variety of companies. Activities such as personnel, shipping and receiving, sales, and customer services are intimately associated in the sense that they contribute to the success of the main business of the enterprise—to sell merchandise. The inclusion of customer services is a happy solution of the difficult problem of carrying out these activities impartially and with justice to both the company and the customer. The customer seems to be the key to the way activities are grouped when the things a company does for him are managed by a single division head.[1] The policies governing the return of merchandise and the servicing of company products can go unchallenged as an effective dominion of a customer service organization. What are the circumstances that will determine the degree that will give the best overall yield for enterprise expenditure for customer development in regard to its products and services? It may be best that this question not be asked. Since, so long as service activities remain undifferentiated or are scattered throughout the enterprise structure, questions of good organization practice in respect to them either do not arise or are considered relatively minor in importance. But, let's examine the *Training Services* to be performed.

FUNCTIONS OF TRAINING PROGRAMS

A training program concerns itself with the development of skills, knowledge and attitudes. These three factors make up a training program, whether it is directed toward workers, supervisors, executives, or customers. For the purpose of administration, therefore, it is important to comprehend and plan the training program in each of these functional divisions.

In companies which have a full, integrated training program, sections are categorized in the following manner:

1. *Employee Training.* This program includes all types of job training and education offered to employees below the supervisory level.

2. *Supervisor Training.* This area of the training program stresses heavily the skills, knowledge, and attitudes necessary to a supervisor.

3.   *Executive Training.* This generally differs from supervisor development mainly in breadth and depth.

4.   *Customer Training.* This program includes all manner of training designed for persons requiring skills and knowledge about the company's products or services.

One of the paradoxes of the training movement is that such categorization, in general use, continues in spite of the universal objection to artifical distinctions between employee and supervisor, supervisor and manager, labor and management, and company and customer. Recognizing that this traditional classification is forced, it can be understood why many training programs could actually cut across all organizational lines and integrate with employee, supervisor, executive, and customer training.

EMPLOYEE TRAINING: SYNONYM FOR CUSTOMER TRAINING

Most companies (the top executives, really) feel that for the sake of organizational clarity, employee training includes all manner of training designed for employees—the workers of the company. The programs must deal *only* with the development in the employee of specific skills and abilities necessary to the successful performance of his job. The range of subjects is as great and as varied as the jobs involved in business and industry.

These same executives reflect that the organizational structure is sound if another agency, with the same company, is responsible for the skill and knowledge development of the user of their product or service. They dub this agency *CUSTOMER TRAINING.*

Identity of purpose between employee and customer training

organizations has largely been replaced by disparity of interest and even active hostility, each toward the other. Lack of faith on both sides of the barricade of conflicting interest has led to a scramble for dominance within the enterprise, bolstered by controls and guarantees. In short, the organizational system becomes a house divided against itself. The condition becomes so grave, at times, that it must be remedied at the top.

It is quite possible to eliminate bureaucracy, remove faults and still have a strife-torn training organization. It is also possible to improve the efficiency and the morale of many an ailing enterprise without making radical changes in the organization. The primary need is to prepare personnel to function well with understanding within the framework of their situation.

Bertrand Russell[2] presents a point of view which may, in part, explain the cause for the schism between these two organizations. He states, "Since it is natural to energetic men to love power, it may be assumed that officials in the great majority of cases will wish to have more power than they ought to have." This philosophy also gives part of the reason for duplication of effort, poor utilization of manpower, and waste of materials and facilities in programs other than training. This is why it is important for the business enterprise to be well organized, with all activities clearly spelled out.

There is no need for a separate organization structure for training programs, and the company would benefit by reduced costs in manpower (fewer instructor classifications), facilities (less classroom space) and materials (reduced duplication of effort). Above all, this reasonable approach toward training will help the business meet its competition with a higher level of effectiveness, which is one of the prime responsibilities of the management of any company.

WHO'S RESPONSIBLE?

Establishing responsibility for training in a business enterprise is not a simple matter. It is rather difficult to quarrel with the idea that training should be a line responsibility. How much management expects its line supervisors to do in training depends upon how it generally divides responsibility for its other personnel functions.

Most line supervisors jealously guard their prerogatives, and have little or no desire to relinquish any part of their responsibility. They claim that *they* must accomplish the total job of subordinate development. The unfortunate fact is that training is only a part of the whole job of supervision, and that employees need development on a continuous basis. Employee development, therefore, by line supervision in a formal organized manner is neglected. The most common excuse is that they do not have enough time to train every employee and perform their other supervisory duties. In an environment such as this, a new hire often feels like a fifth wheel, and he begins to develop frustration and fear.

If training can be thought of as a staff function, then the responsibility of personnel development can be delegated. This type of responsibility determination can be accomplished by an upper management edict.

The concept of the training department operating as a staff function with no power beyond weak and apologetic advice is a poor one indeed. If management expects results from the department, it must give responsibility accompanied by authority. This authority must include planning, controlling, coordinating, and administering of all education and training activities.

WHERE ON THE ORGANIZATION CHART?

Training is a service department. Although much controversy occurs over where such a function should report, traditionally training reports to a personnel or industrial relations function. If we buy the idea that training is strictly a service organization, maybe we should break with tradition.

The major consideration for organizational placement must be that the training organization be placed in a function that handles activities similar to those of training and has similar objectives. This concept emphasizes that when activities that have common objectives are grouped together under one administrator, maximum utilization of available resources is attained.

A second consideration for placement is that training should be organizationally placed where it can serve ALL units of the enterprise: production, service, sales, office, legal, research, traffic, quality control, finance, etc. If the training function is centered in any one of these areas, it may be inclined to devote more attention there and "find" it difficult to serve the other units.

Regardless of his placement on the organization chart, the training director must be a member of the top echelon. Top management must recognize the fact that he is dealing with matters of vital importance to the company. Too often the training director is outside the "in" group. A training director cannot plan training to meet a need known only to the top echelon of a company's management. A training director who is a member of this upper echelon is the exception rather than the rule.

Functional Divisions of a Typical Training Department

We can add to this chart by listing the important courses (subject matter) through which these functions (objectives) can be achieved. Courses in company history, organization, policy, and services help considerably in the orientation of new hires and supervisors. Training in principles of organization, planning, staffing, controlling, cost control, and job evaluation help to develop management skills. Training in the skills and information required to perform the job will help to develop the worker's technical proficiency. Since the training department has instructors technically qualified to train employees to assemble the company's product, how much more will be required to have them qualified to train customers to disassemble that same product for service and repair? *(Your answer!)*

In accomplishment of the foregoing, subject matter becomes even more important than a superficial observation might lead us to conclude. If the subject matter is the prime consideration, then, the type of attendee is relevant only from the consideration as to who will pay for his attendance—the company if *employee;* someone else if *customer.* Customer training *now* becomes an exercise in accounting.

SUMMARY

If a company is to attain its organizational objectives, it must have a well-trained work force. The employee training division can aid in this attainment. If training is accepted with the same confidence as are other staff functions, such as engineering, legal, sales and service and quality control, then a healthy relationship will be maintained. Only resentment based on supposed interference from customer service people causes conflict between them and employee development people. A recognition that the training division is just as concerned with company success as any other division will do much toward the achievement of a healthy relationship.

Formalized training programs of any kind are better than haphazard training. A company's training effort must be integrated with all the rest of its efforts. Training must be given the same attention as the other major business functions if the company is to achieve optimum success and maintain its competitive position.

Actually, training organizations differ from company to company. This difference is based partly on the needs within the individual company. The most frequent approach to the organization problem is to place the training director under the supervision of the head of the personnel activity in the company concerned. But, the *most* important aspect of training division organization that must be considered is its status in relation to other staff and service activities of the business.

We must keep in mind that the function of the training director is to promote the integration of training activities so that a given program can be accomplished efficiently and economically.

REFERENCES

1.   Koontz, Harold & Cyril O'Donnell. *Principles of Management.* New York: McGraw-Hill Book Company, 1968.

2.   Russell, Bertrand. *Authority and the Individual.* Boston: Beacon Press, 1960.